Blasted with Antiquity

Blasted with Antiquity
Old Age and the Consolations of Literature

David Ellis

The Lutterworth Press

The Lutterworth Press

P.O. Box 60
Cambridge
CB1 2NT
United Kingdom

www.lutterworth.com
publishing@lutterworth.com

Paperback ISBN: 978 0 7188 9718 5
PDF ISBN: 978 0 7188 9717 8
ePub ISBN: 978 0 7188 9716 1

British Library Cataloguing in Publication Data
A record is available from the British Library

First published by The Lutterworth Press, 2023

Copyright © David Ellis, 2023

All rights reserved. No part of this edition may be reproduced, stored electronically or in any retrieval system, or transmitted in any form or by any means, electronic, mechanical, photocopying, recording, or otherwise, without prior written permission from the Publisher (permissions@lutterworth.com).

Contents

List of Illustrations   vii

Note on Referencing   ix

1	Introduction	1
2	Retirement	15
3	Ageing, Decrepitude and the Wisdom of the Elders	27
4	Self-consciousness and Sex	39
5	Family Matters	51
6	Leaving One's Mark	63
7	Will Power	75
8	Nostalgia	89
9	Taking Stock	101
10	Doctoring and Dying	113
11	Ending Up	125
12	Postscript: On 'the Stages of Life'	139

List of Works Cited   151

Acknowledgements   159

Index   161

Contents

List of Illustrations

1.	Goya's satirical sketch of an old man 'still learning'	x
2.	Happy Families: Shakespeare in his Garden	14
3.	Swift's Struldbruggs	26
4.	'Monkey Gland' Treatment	38
5.	*The Cumberland Beggar*	50
6.	Ramesses II	62
7.	*Reading the Will*	74
8.	Recruiting Office, 1914 Source: Mirrorpix	88
9.	*The Last Judgement*	100
10.	*Applying the Leeches* Source: Wellcome Collection, CC-By-4.0	112
11.	*The Death of Addison* Photo credit Ashmolean Museum, Oxford	124
12.	*The Ages of Woman and Death*	138

Note on Referencing

This is not the kind of book which requires detailed referencing. For those in search of bibliographic detail, I have tried to incorporate into my text information that will allow the reader to track my quotations and allusions to the 'list of books cited' on pp. 151-7 and, where that might not be sufficient, I have added the occasional footnote.

Goya's satirical sketch of an old man 'still learning'
Aún Aprendo, c. 1826. Prado Museum, Madrid

1

Introduction

The variety and richness of Falstaff's language is remarkable. Who else could call the disreputable band of robbers young Prince Hal will join 'Diana's foresters, gentlemen of the shade, minions of the moon', or protest, when this same prince is mocking him for being fat, that at Hal's age he was not 'an eagle's talon in the waist' and could have 'crept into any alderman's thumb ring'? This unlikely claim is followed by one of Falstaff's jokes: 'A plague of sighing and grief!' he says, 'It blows a man up like a bladder', as if the heavier breathing associated with sighing acted like a pump.

Despite unpromising titles, the first two parts of *Henry the Fourth* combine to form one of the great works of world literature and Falstaff's lines are far from being the only ones in these plays which are memorable. There is, for example, a speech of the Lord Chief Justice in *King Henry IV: Part 2* that always impressed me, even before I reached an age to appreciate it fully. When he is not distracted by more important affairs, this character has been pursuing Falstaff for various crimes and misdemeanours and, in the second scene of the second play, will not be fobbed off with 'You that are old consider not the capacities of us that are young.' Exasperated by the outrageous implications of this claim, the Lord Chief Justice explodes into:

> Do you set down your name in the scroll of youth, that are written down old with all the characters of age? Have you not a moist eye, a dry hand, a yellow cheek, a white beard, a decreasing leg, an increasing belly? Is not your voice broken, your wind short, your chin double, your wit single, and every

part of you blasted with antiquity? And will you yet call yourself young? Fie, fie, fie, Sir John!'

Here is a list of the stigmata of old age, delivered with impressive and enjoyable force. Not all its items register now as they would have done in the late sixteenth century and when today, for instance, men are no longer obliged to dress like male ballet dancers. A 'decreasing leg' is not such a problem if few people are going to be in a position to observe it, although T.S. Eliot does have his Prufrock worry that people will notice, not only that he is losing his hair, but 'how his arms and legs are thin!'

Elsewhere in his plays, Shakespeare adds to the Lord Chief Justice's list of the disadvantages of ageing and many modern readers could no doubt want to add to it also. A question that puzzles me is why my mind should have been determined to retain this speech when its implications are so disheartening. Why also, that is, although I enjoy all Falstaff's efforts to demonstrate that he is a fit companion for two men about town like Hal and Poins, as full of health and vigour as they are – 'They hate us youth!' he famously shouts, as he leads his attack on the travellers – I also relish those exchanges he has with Doll Tearsheet in act 2 scene 4 of *King Henry IV: Part 2*. This is after Hal and Poins have contrived to overhear the unflattering remarks they rightly believed Falstaff would make about them when he thought they were out of earshot. When are you going to leave off riotous living, Doll asks him, and 'patch up thine old body for heaven?' 'Peace, good Doll!' he replies, 'Do not speak like a death's head. Do not bid me remember mine end.' When she insists that the kisses she is giving him come from a sincere heart, he can only reply, in what increasingly seems to me one of the most poignant moments in Shakespeare, 'I am old, I am old.'

Although the lessons one could learn about old age from great literature are often unpalatable, they have a linguistic or dramatic value that makes them easier to digest. While avoiding as far as possible speaking like a death's head, I try in what follows to negotiate the encounter with various aspects of ageing through a number of literary texts I happen to admire. My choice of texts is largely based on years of teaching these works in a way that is now dropping out of fashion, so that this book is also a requiem for a style of thinking and feeling that is fast disappearing, in the universities, if not in the world at large. When I first began a course in literature at university, my father asked what I was studying and, after I had told him it was 'English', wondered, with far more puzzlement than sarcasm, whether that was not something I already knew. In those days, however, there was a belief abroad that to help a number of young people to read, in a careful manner, what were then widely regarded as the classics of English literature was to perform a public service. At the lowest level, this was because grappling with the subtleties of a great writer's use of the language was believed to make students more adept at detecting and denouncing its misuse in public and commercial life. An offshoot of this conviction had been a book used in schools entitled *Reading and Discrimination*, which offered to help pupils recognise and resist those black arts of language advertisers employ to persuade the public to buy their goods. It had been put together by Denys Thompson at a time when there was a growing unease about the way commercial interests were infiltrating more and more branches of the entertainment industry, sport and public life generally. 'Good luck with that' might have been the appropriate comment on this worthy effort to put a finger in the dyke, had that fine example of modern irony been available at the time.

It was not entirely foolish to believe that university students had to be helped to read, that 'English' was something they did not already know. Not all literary texts, and those from the past especially, are immediately accessible to all native speakers and, if they do not call for some kind of training before they reveal themselves fully, they at least require habituation. Their readers need to have the kind of space and time universities can provide to get used to unfamiliar locutions so that they can reap the benefits of a gratification which is by no means always instant. Gratification it nonetheless is, not only in the pleasures of language but also in the enjoyment or satisfaction that comes from having so many different aspects of human experience explored with the kind of intelligence certainly different from that of a philosopher or sociologist, but, in my view, of at least equal value.

Old age is one of those aspects and, as it becomes a reality for an increasing percentage of the population, it is hardly surprising that there should be an increase in those wanting to write about it. Judging by the library shelves, a majority of the more academic studies of old age do not emanate from literature departments. A key text has been a work of over 500 pages by Pat Thane called *Old Age in English History: Past Experiences and Present Issues*. Despite its title, this book begins with Greece and Rome but then moves swiftly on to the Middle Ages and surveys expertly, and in great detail, the treatment of the old in England from that point on, to the accompaniment of a considerable number of statistical tables. At its start, Thane refers to anxieties being expressed at her time of writing about the rising number of old people as a proportion of the population as a whole. This is now more than 20 years ago and, while that proportion continues to grow, so do the anxieties. In 2019, Camilla Cavendish, a former advisor to David Cameron when he was British Prime Minister, published a book called *Extra Time: Ten Lessons for an Ageing World*, which begins with a series of graphs demonstrating that 'by 2020, for the first time in history, there will be more people on the planet over 65 than under 5. More grandparents than grandchildren.' With younger people in this country having to fund with their taxes pensions of a kind they themselves are unlikely to enjoy, Cavendish is interested in what can be done in the political sphere to protect a social contract which, she writes, 'is being stretched to breaking point by the changing ratio of young to old'.

One obvious danger of the situation Cavendish describes is indeed the rise of an enmity between the generations that is perhaps always lurking, and which Thane illustrates by reference to English peasant farmers from the Middle Ages. When they became too old and weak to work their land, some of them transferred it to their children on the understanding that they would be provided with a stipulated amount of income, food or accommodation. Yet when harvests were poor, the children could bitterly resent having to fulfil these obligations and, in extreme cases, find ways of doing away with those extra mouths to feed. There is a sociological reality here that is in the background to *King Lear* and now seems to us both alien and repellent. In an interview she recorded with the distinguished gerontologist and writer Raymond Tallis for her book *About Time: Growing Old Disgracefully*, Irma Kurtz pointed out that official screening for breast cancer tends to stop at 70, even though it is after this age that its incidence is greatest. This is presumably because of a cost-benefit analysis which indicates that limited resources are better spent on those with a decent life expectancy; and yet what it amounts to, in Kurtz's view, is 'a subliminal euthanasia at work among us' and therefore a translation into modern, institutional terms of those feelings that in the past occasionally led hard-pressed peasants to do away with their old folk.[1]

Thane does occasionally quote literary sources in her descriptive survey, but she is not very interested in them as ways of highlighting and then pondering the individual ramifications of old age. This is also broadly true of her successors, either in social history or the so-called

---

1. She was, of course, writing before the recent pandemic and the measures taken which, it could be argued (and occasionally is), involved sacrificing the interests of the young so that the old could enjoy a few more years of life.

harder sciences. The scholars from the academic 'English' community who have tackled this subject have usually confined themselves to what was said about old age by authors within a certain period. This was true, for example, of Nina Taunton in her *Fictions of Old Age in Early Modern Literature and Culture* and Karen Chase in *The Victorians and Old Age*, while Devoney Looser adopted a limit or boundary additional to the temporal one in her *Women Writers and Old Age in Great Britain, 1750-1850*. Limits were clear enough in the title of Jacob Jewusiak's *Aging, Duration, and the English Novel: Growing Old from Dickens to Woolf* and Christopher Martin's *Constituting Old Age in Early Modern Literature from Queen Elizabeth to* King Lear, while Heike Hartung's *Ageing, Gender and Illness in Anglophone Literature: Narrating Age in the Bildungsroman* begins its story in the late eighteenth century. Needless to say, I have found useful suggestions or challenges in all these books, and several more like them, but my own approach is thematic in that I have taken various features of old age and tried to discuss them in relation to the work of a number of writers from many different periods whose writings I consider 'an imaginative resource for understanding variations in the meaning of the experience of ageing in society'. This is how Mike Hepworth neatly put it in his *Stories of Ageing*, although he is a social scientist whose 'stories' are to be found only in the novels and popular culture of the second half of the twentieth century, and who studies these 'within a "symbolic interactionist" framework', symbolic interactionism being 'one of the branches of sociology that places a high value on the role of the imagination in the development of the concept of the self'.

This book begins with thoughts on retirement, especially as it affects men and their families (that women who have in the past spent their lives as housewives seldom have the opportunity to retire is an injustice Thane curtly registers). It goes on to consider the physical decay often associated with old age, no matter how valiantly or vainly it may be resisted; and then its relation to questions of sex and self-consciousness. At what point does it become appropriate to give up any pretension to sexual allure or sexual prowess? The difference having a family makes is next on my agenda along with the pressing need many people feel to leave behind some record of their having existed, apart from (or instead of) their children. How reasonable is it for people to be concerned about their 'legacy' when either its material – in the case of a monument of some kind, for example – or merely intellectual survival will be subject to conditions over which they will have no control? There are many respects in which growing old can mean a loss of not only status but also power, while one way of reasserting this, both before as well as after death, is through a will. That wills are remarkably frequent as plot devices in many literary works prompts me to consider their effectiveness as a means of allowing the old to maintain their grasp on the future.

The retrospection that is such a prominent part of old age can often take the form of nostalgia. Although some recent work in social psychology has sought to demonstrate how much positive value it can have, nostalgia has usually been regarded with disapproval in literary circles, even though it is ubiquitous in both books and life. Distinct from it is that operation of taking stock of one's past which, for sanguine temperaments, can become a matter for geriatric self-satisfaction but, in other cases, for distress and guilt. How best to acknowledge and expiate this guilt is a problem with which many writers have been concerned, especially in their autobiographies, and which can become particularly acute as they are increasingly obliged to look forward as well as back. It is then that they, and the rest of us, are more likely to be involved with the medical profession and to have to come to terms with the fact that the common talk of 'surviving old age', which Edward Enfield relies on for the title of a collection of short pieces from the *Oldie* magazine (*Old Age and How to Survive It*), can have no logical justification. In one gloomy aspect of the Christian tradition, the whole of life is a preparation for death but for most people that process kicks in rather late, if at all, while how best to handle it is not usually evident or clear. In my penultimate chapter, I consider the circumstances or mythology surrounding a few well-known last moments and attempt myself to have a final say (although only on some of the topics I have been discussing!). There is then a postscript in which I investigate briefly the traditional seven, four or is it three 'ages of man' – as well as of women, of course – and ask a few questions about the habit of dividing a life up in this way.

Relying on literary texts as an aid to thoughts about ageing would seem to be an obvious move but I am not aware of many others who have made it. Someone who might have been expected to adopt this approach, but didn't, is one of the few commentators with an international reputation to have addressed the subject at any length. Published in 1970, Simone de Beauvoir's *Old Age* is described by Thane as 'relentlessly gloomy' and 'tendentious'. What prompts this last word is perhaps its author's repeated assertion that, in a capitalist country like France, the old are treated scandalously although, in fact, her book is for the most part very much like Thane's in not being a polemic at all but rather a long and impressively scholarly review of how the old have been treated throughout history. On the rare occasions it does become analytic rather than descriptive, de Beauvoir tends to turn neither to literature, nor to those remarkable literary gifts which make her own account of how her mother died, with its ironic reference in its title to an easy death (*Une Mort très douce*), so moving, but to her background in philosophy. She considers at one point, for example, how important the idea of reciprocity is in society, that kind of understanding which one might see exemplified in the care the young are often prepared to give to the old as a return for what they received when they were not in a position to look after themselves, and the survival of which Camilla Cavendish is so worried about. Reciprocity, de Beauvoir writes, recalling the work of her life-long companion Jean-Paul Sartre:

> implies (1) that the other should be the means of a transcendent end; (2) that I should acknowledge him as a praxis at the same time that I integrate him as an object in my project as a whole; (3) that I recognize his motion towards his ends in the movement by means of which I project myself towards mine; (4) that I see myself as an object and instrument of those ends through the very act which constitutes him as an objective instrument for my ends.

Anyone who has struggled with Sartre's *Critique of Dialectical Reason*, or his *Being and Nothingness*, will know that this is not nonsense; and I am also aware that, as BBC commentators are obliged to say, other philosophers are available. Yet, whether in French or any other language, there are several of the latter who give an equally strong sense as de Beauvoir in the passage above that there is sometimes a hostile antithesis between philosophical and literary ways of talking about the human condition.

That philosophers do not have a lot to say of value about old age and ageing, however they choose to express it, would be an absurd position to take and I refer briefly to at least two of them later; but my own major focus is on the contribution made by writers, in both the records they or others have left of their own lives and in what they have otherwise written. This is in contrast to Helen Small who, although a professor of English, admitted in her introduction to *The Long Life* (2007) that her book was 'an attempt to show what might be required if we are to become more seriously philosophical about old age', and that her approach gave 'a structural priority to philosophy'. While not wanting to do that, I am aware that my use of literary texts in this enquiry may look to some both arbitrary and amateurish. That another book could have been written along the same lines as this one but using different examples is so irrefutable that it strikes me more as a fact of life than a potential criticism, as does what would now be known as the Euro-centrism of those examples. (The books I happen to know have little to say on what it feels like to be old in Africa, Asia and other non-European parts of the world.) On the second issue of amateurism, I realise that I could be accused of sometimes citing certain texts without their appropriate historical and cultural context. The people who used to believe a degree in English was largely a matter of giving students the opportunity to read a great many books thought to be worthwhile were perfectly aware that there would be occasions when they would need the kind of information or knowledge that universities are traditionally in the business of supplying. This could well be about how both the historical and linguistic contexts in which works were written have changed over time; but these teachers were less worried about my knowing too little on that score than of the danger of substituting knowledge *about* a text for a reasonably intimate familiarity with it. They liked to recall the reply Matthew Arnold gave in *On Translating Homer* after he had been accused of knowing too little about the subject to be an adequate critic of it. 'Perverse as it seems to say so', Arnold wrote, 'I sometimes find myself wishing, when dealing with these matters of poetical criticism, that my ignorance were even greater than it is.' This was because 'poetical criticism' required a usually fine balance, one that 'erudition' could easily destroy. He went on to recall, with that irony for which he was notorious and which once led Robert Bridges to call him 'Mr Kidglove Cocksure', how the Duke of Wellington had said of a certain peer that 'it was a great pity his education had been so far too much for his abilities', and claim that he himself was always apprehensive, in dealing with poetry, that even the little he knew might put him in the same position.

In her study of old age and the Victorians, Karen Chase claims that Betty Higden, an old woman who plays a minor role in Dickens' *Our Mutual Friend*, has been 'long anathematized by contemporary moderns who find her portrait sentimental and her obsession with the workhouse melodramatic'; however, Chase insists, she 'is none of these things when placed, or replaced, in her historical/institutional moment'. What then follows are numerous and quite lengthy details about the operation of the poor law in nineteenth-century England. In all literary commentary there is an uneasy compromise to be struck between how certain texts seem to us today and the impression they are likely to have made on their original readers. Interesting though they are, what Chase's details illustrate is the tendency 'English' has had, ever since it was established as a university subject, and the qualification for teaching it became a research degree, to slide towards cultural studies. Although there will always be cases where historical or linguistic context is so important it cannot be ignored, I have chosen an organisation in this book that allows me to concentrate chiefly, if not exclusively, on what certain, mostly well-known texts can mean for us now; so that, for example, I think of *Martin Chuzzlewit*'s Sarah Gamp, who is a character Chase links with Betty Higden and considers in relation to the information she herself provides about domiciliary nursing in the nineteenth century, not principally for what she tells us about her times but as one of Dickens' great comic creations. Not so much, that is, as an item in the debate that was going on in Dickens' time, and which is still going on, about the standard of care available to the sick and old, but, above all, as the woman who, reporting on her account of her family circumstances for her quite possibly mythical friend Mrs Harris, refers to her dead children as having had 'damp doorstops settled on their lungs', and to one of her ex-husbands as having been disabled so that now 'there's a wooden leg gone likewise home to its account, which in its constancy of walkin' into wine vaults, and never comin' out again 'til fetched by force, was quite as weak as flesh, if not weaker'. Cultural historians reasonably question why major works of art should be more significant and useful as evidence, more representative, than the minor ones, and it is true that period studies in English tend to stray into relatively unfamiliar areas (Devoney Looser's women writers, for example, include Fanny Burney and Jane Austen but also Catherine Macaulay, Hester Piozzi, Letitia Barbauld and Jane Porter). Since I am not limiting myself to any particular period in what follows, the writers I consider are, on the whole, those which most people in the West would think worth listening to whatever the topic, even if they do not all exhibit the same astonishing linguistic virtuosity as Dickens in his portrait of Mrs Gamp.

What Dickens is able to do with the English language could often be said to gladden the heart and make you thankful to be alive. I put it in this somewhat melodramatic fashion because I am aware that another charge that might be brought against this book is that it is hardly designed to make its older readers feel more cheerful. Helen Small shows herself aware of this problem when she suggests in her book *The Long Life* that, historically speaking, accounts of old age have tended to be more negative than positive and that they have thus 'offended most recent writers about ageing, especially when they start to look like biological essentialism'. This last term is usually associated with discussions of gender but its appearance here is presumably in implicit contrast with the idea that 'old age' is socially constructed. That in many ways it certainly is gives us reason for optimism in that the social and political circumstances which give rise to a society's concept of what it means to be old are not set in stone and can be altered; yet it is surely also the case that there are a number of biological processes that are ineluctable and bound to give a somewhat sombre colouring to any attempt to discuss growing old. The hope is that, although the paraphraseable content of what my chosen writers have had to say on the topic is often depressing, it can be balanced, to some extent at least, by the pleasure generated from the ways they say it.

I find a very minor illustration of this possibility in those words from Shakespeare I have chosen for my title. As anyone who has ever put pen to paper knows, titles are difficult and I have looked with envy at those adopted for a number of publications within this general field. D.J. Enright was a minor poet from the fairly recent past whom I happened to have known and admired greatly, not only for his literary abilities but also his integrity (the life choices he made meant that his last years were spent in comparative poverty). When he was already ill, he wrote a prose memoir that appeared just after his death and to which he gave the splendid title *Injury Time*. The final word here also features in the title of a work by Maurice Charney that deals exclusively with old age as it appears in Shakespeare's plays and is called *Wrinkled Deep in Time*. Those words are, of course, Cleopatra's and remarkably striking. Almost equally so are those of Lear when he is describing how he intends to transfer the responsibilities of kingship to 'younger strengths' while 'we / Unburdened crawl toward death'.

Crawling towards death is a memorable expression, in part because it evokes the common idea of old age as a second childhood equivalent in so many unfortunate ways to the first but with the major difference that no one ever grows up and out of it. Yet, when I was seriously and no doubt foolishly considering it as a title, I remembered the difficulty I had in finding something suitable for a book I wrote a long time ago on Wordsworth's great autobiographical poem, *The Prelude*. My focus had then been on those traumatic episodes in Wordsworth's childhood that he called 'spots of time', one of which took place when he was six and riding with a servant in the Lake District. Finding himself at one point alone, he led his horse into a hollow and discovered there an old gibbet where the executed body of a murderer had once been hung in chains. The apparatus had mostly 'moulder'd down' but the dead man's name had been carved into the turf nearby and kept fresh by the locals. Rapidly climbing back up from the hollow, Wordsworth vividly remembers having seen, 'A naked pool that lay beneath the hills, / The Beacon on the summit, and, more near, / A Girl, who bore a Pitcher on her head /

And seem'd with difficult steps to force her way / Against the blowing wind.' This was, as he says, an ordinary sight but he felt it would take more resources than he had available, or than anyone else possessed, to describe 'the visionary dreariness' with which it was invested. 'Well, there you are', said a witty friend with whom I was discussing this episode, 'call your book *The Visionary Dreariness* and watch how quickly it disappears off the shelves'. Crawling towards death might not be quite as off-putting as visionary dreariness but I can see that it might well have given the wrong impression, however much one insists on 'unburdened', or suggests that these are the words of a man given to self-dramatisation.[2] That Othello is given to self-dramatisation was what was often said in my youth and I was conscious even then of how difficult it might be to distinguish the actor playing a role from the role-playing of his character. Still, the difference is clear enough in someone like Falstaff who loves to take on various personae: 'Before I knew thee, Hal, I knew nothing; and now am I, if a man should speak truly, little better than one of the wicked.'

Because there is no reason why old age should reduce us to all fours and, as the French cabaret artist Maurice Chevalier is reputed to have said, it is at least better than the alternative, this book now has a title less forbidding than the one I first contemplated, if, for many, only marginally so. Throughout it, I have tried to maintain a focus on what would generally be considered old although in periods when life expectancy was so much less than it is now that word can often have a different meaning, and indeed it is one which alters its sense considerably according to various cultural, political and even psychological contexts. Lord Byron, for example, first became a celebrity through the invention of a persona (Childe Harold) who, while still in his early twenties, was old before his time, someone who believed that he had already anticipated all that future experience could offer and had nothing to look forward to. As he turned 30, and detected his first grey hairs, Byron himself was convinced that, since his lifespan would be short (he did, in fact, die at 36), he was already in his last phase. There are figures who knew that they had a terminal illness and, with rather more justification than Byron, had this same feeling even though they were not old in the usual sense. I have included consideration of one or two of these, from either fiction or real life, because the problems they had to face are very similar to those of people who have reached three score and ten, or some similarly advanced

---

2. Since writing these words my attention has been directed to Markus Poetzsch, *The Visionary Dreariness: Readings in Romanticism's Quotidian Sublime* (London: Routledge, 2006). I hope it did well.

stage, and find themselves contemplating their end. Mainly, however, this is about what it used to be considered polite to call the elderly, a rather better word perhaps than those that have been concocted around 'senior'. In former times, old age could be something of a distinction because there was relatively so little of it. Anyone who wanders into the centre of a small English town during an ordinary working day, or has occasion to visit a doctor's waiting room in the afternoon, might well feel that an invading alien force has now taken over, not always so steady on its feet, nimble or sharp-eyed, but compensating for these disadvantages by sheer force of numbers, and sometimes stubbornly reclaiming the pavement from terrorising youth on bicycles with its mobility scooters. Yet there were enough of these people around in the past for what writers said about them, or what the older ones among them said about themselves, to have some relevance still.

Happy Families: Shakespeare in his Garden
Lithograph by Charles Dudley Tennant (1867-1952)

2

Retirement

It may only be since the introduction of state pensions, which in Britain dates from the beginning of the twentieth century, that there has been a close link between retirement and old age so that it now makes sense to talk, as we so frequently do, of the 'early' variety. Before that period, the word sometimes implied not so much that people were reaching the end of their useful working life but that they had taken a conscious decision to withdraw from the stresses and strains of society. In his *Lives of the Poets*, Dr Johnson describes how, after the seventeenth-century writer Abraham Cowley had failed to secure the preferment he expected on the restoration of Charles II, and after one of his plays had been badly received, a 'vehement desire of retirement now came again upon him'. He therefore retreated to the country but 'wisely went only so far from the bustle of life', Johnson sardonically adds, 'as he might easily find his way back, when solitude should grow tedious.'

As this example illustrates, retirement usually meant a move from town to country and, although there may be cases of people who spend all their working lives in a rural environment and then retire to a flat in some great city, it still often does. The idea that there are far fewer vexations in rural than urban life goes back at least as far as the Latin poet Horace's tale of the town and country mouse, if not beyond. Johnson was a confirmed townie who is well-known for having said that anyone who was tired of London must be tired of life and who regarded the attractions of rural retreats with deep scepticism. When his friend Richard Savage encountered financial difficulties so severe that a group of admirers offered him a small pension on condition that he would leave London and go to live in a part of the country where life was much cheaper, Johnson urged him to stay put and, by a more resolute exertion of his literary abilities, endeavour to support himself. Alas Savage, Johnson says, was seduced by a notion he had in his head of the 'calm of a cottage' and could not bear to deprive himself of the opportunity of 'listening without interruption to the melody of the nightingale, which he believed was to be heard from every bramble, and which he did not fail to mention as a very important part of the happiness of a country life'.

Of course, for writers like Cowley and Savage, or artists of any kind, retirement does not necessarily mean what it tends to mean for the rest of us. In Proust's *Within a Budding Grove* (the second volume of *Remembrance of Things Past*), the narrator meets a famous painter called Elstir who has retired into 'unsociable isolation'. No doubt, Proust's narrator speculates, Elstir 'had at first thought with pleasure, even in his solitude, that, thanks to his work, he was addressing from a distance, was imbuing with a loftier idea of himself, those who had misunderstood or offended him', that he was dedicating his work 'to certain people as a sort of new approach whereby, without actually seeing him, they would be brought to love him, admire him, talk about him'. This is clearly a special kind of retirement or withdrawal and yet, the text goes on, as time passed Elstir's practice of solitude began to give him a disinterested love of it so that he grew reconciled to a lack of any kind of public significance and his retirement came to be much like anyone else's.

A seventeenth- or eighteenth-century gentleman did not have to be old to retire but even in those days it was a process more usually belonging to later life, to the autumn Edward Gibbon might be said to be describing when he talks in his *Memoirs* of that 'mature season in which our passions are calmed, our duties fulfilled, our ambitions satisfied, our fame and fortune established on a solid basis', conditions he clearly felt had been more than amply met in his own case. What they suggest is a utopian vision of retirement and one that we have therefore been happy to associate with figures from the past whose achievements make us feel they deserve it. The first biography of Shakespeare was by Nicholas Rowe and appeared in 1709, almost a century after its subject's death when any material that may once have given an accurate, detailed picture of his private life had disappeared. It was Rowe who began the tradition of assuring us that 'the latter part of [Shakespeare's] life was spent, as all men of good sense will wish theirs may be, in ease, retirement and the conversation of friends'. Later, it became customary to link the moment of Shakespeare's return to Stratford, very much a *country* town in his day, to a speech in what was assumed to be his last play. Because of his magical powers, Prospero has been responsible for stage-managing much of the action in *The Tempest* but, towards the end of act 5, he talks of abjuring these, and of breaking his staff or wand as well as drowning his book of spells in the sea. Here, it was thought, we find Shakespeare speaking through his central character and bidding a definitive farewell to the stage.

By the time he wrote *The Tempest*, Shakespeare had certainly made enough money in the theatre to buy both a coat of arms for his family as well as what is usually described as the second largest house in the town where he was born. That is to say that, unlike many of his playwriting contemporaries, most of whom died poor and early, he had every prospect of a comfortable last phase. Reunited with his wife after the long years of separation his work in London had required, he had the satisfaction of seeing both his daughters married, one of them to a doctor (every ageing man's dream, especially if the doctor happens to be a gerontologist). His writing had brought him a degree of fame so that, in addition to the locals, those friends with whom Rowe imagines him conversing could well have included visitors from the capital such as Ben Jonson, the man who, when the first collected edition of Shakespeare's plays was published seven years after his death in 1616, was to provide such a fulsome tribute.

In its idealisation of his last years, Shakespeare's retirement became a model to which Rowe's 'men of good sense' could aspire, even when what they had to look back on were achievements hardly as impressive as *Macbeth* or *King Lear*. In the many later accounts of Shakespeare's life, writers, and also painters, liked to imagine him strolling in the orchard they pictured as being attached to his large house. This may be in part because some of them still had at the back of their minds what Horace says about the delights of his Sabine farm, but the appeal of quiet, peaceful retirement in a country setting has always been very strong. Gainsborough, for example, looked forward to the day when he could abandon portrait painting and, taking his viol da gamba, 'walk off to some sweet village where I can paint landscapes and enjoy the tag end of life in quietness and ease'.[1]

In the nineteenth century, an orchard became an integral part of the picture of Shakespeare's ease, perhaps because of the way it subconsciously

---

1. Gainsborough's remark about decamping to a 'sweet village' was conveyed to me by a friend but it is quoted by Mary Cyr in her 'Carl Friedrich Abel's Solos: A Musical Offering to Gainsborough?', *The Musical Times*, Vol. 128, no. 1732 (June 1987), pp. 317-21.

offered the opportunity of associating his last years with wholly natural processes of growth and decay. This was not so much in the disillusioned spirit of his own Touchstone who, in *As You Like It*, is observed by Jaques looking at his timepiece and overheard saying that, whereas it is now ten o'clock, an hour ago it was nine and soon will be eleven so that 'from hour to hour, we ripe and ripe, / And then, from hour to hour, we rot and rot'; but rather in that (to move rapidly forward in time!) of D.H. Lawrence in a poem entitled 'Beautiful Old Age'. If people lived without accepting lies, Lawrence says in this late piece, 'they would ripen like apples, and be scented like pippins in their old age'. Coming to their 'wrinkled ripe fulfilment', they would presumably then float gently to the ground, although this is hardly what usually happens, a fact that Lawrence, who died of tuberculosis when he was 44, was in a good position to recognise.

We cannot know for sure that this picture, which so many people had in their heads, of Shakespeare strolling comfortably in his orchard is false, or at least seriously incomplete, because the documentary record is so sparse. It might have happened that way just as today there are certainly people who retire to their bungalows in the country, cultivate their gardens, in both the literal and Voltairean sense of that expression, and, after fifteen or so happy and pain-free years (punctuated by occasional trips to warmer climes), die peacefully in their sleep. Gibbon is someone who gives the impression in his autobiography of being happy in retirement, contently resting on his laurels; but there are at least indications that in this he was not at all like Shakespeare. In the first place, *The Tempest* was not his last play. At least three others followed, written in collaboration with a member or members of his theatre company. Secondly, although it is true that Shakespeare's elder daughter, Susannah, was safely married to a doctor, the younger one, Judith, only found a partner a few months before her father's death. He was a man called Thomas Quiney, the son of one of his old friends. It is comforting when a dying man can leave this world with his children securely settled in life but, shortly after the marriage, Quiney was obliged to confess in an ecclesiastical court to having recently had 'carnal copulation' with a certain Margaret Wheeler who had died in childbirth a few weeks earlier. This is thought by many to explain the somewhat convoluted arrangements Shakespeare appears to have made in his will to deprive his new son-in-law of too easy an access to Judith's inheritance. That cannot be known for certain but there are enough surviving details to suggest that family life must not have been for Shakespeare, in his last years, entirely smooth sailing.

A notorious feature of the will is that Shakespeare's wife only appears in it is as the beneficiary of his second-best bed, a gesture that raises doubts about his affection for her, not entirely dispelled by the fact that beds were expensive commodities in Jacobean England, or that the second-best bed could well have been the one he and Ann slept in, the best, or better of them, being reserved for visitors. How he got on with her in his final years is something we can never know but it may not have helped that, according to many authorities, she was more or less illiterate. Another feature of the will is its distinctly spidery signature. This has been taken as suggestive of a man who had suffered some damage to his central nervous system and one possible reason for this, it has been conjectured, was syphilis. The highly dubious logic offered in support of this contention is that there is a great deal about venereal disease in Shakespeare's plays and that, although his doctor son-in-law kept notebooks, there is no mention of Shakespeare in them. Ignoring the possibility that not all the notebooks have survived, some of those who support the syphilis thesis have argued that what they show is how 'decency prevailed over clinical candour'.[2] Arguments like these are hardly likely to shake the conviction that we do not know, and probably never can know, what Shakespeare was suffering from when he died but the signature does give a hint that he was not well and that his retirement might not have been as idyllic as Rowe, and many others after him, implied. Yet, for those in later years who were contemplating retirement, or about to embark upon it, it must have been comforting to imagine that, in this famous instance at least, merit was rewarded and the man who had done so much for British culture passed his last days in peace and contentment.

Imagining that Prospero is speaking for Shakespeare in *The Tempest*, or that the abundance of references to venereal disease in his plays means that he must himself have been a sufferer, are two clear examples of how *not* to compensate for our ignorance of his private life. We know so little about his relationship with his daughters that it would be even more foolish to wonder whether it had any influence on the composition of *King Lear*. The premise of this play is unusual in that monarchs do not often retire, the sixteenth-century head of the Holy Roman Empire, Charles V, who gave up his position in 1556, two years before his death, being a notable exception. That the more usual word in their case is

---

2. The words are those of Anthony Burgess in his biography, *Shakespeare*, but his view is supported by Katherine Duncan-Jones in hers.

'abdicate' is itself an indication of a feeling that monarchs are not usually entitled to abandon their responsibilities, especially when doing so necessitates a division of their kingdoms. At the beginning of the play, Kent and Gloucester note that, as far as Goneril and Regan are concerned, the king's sharing out of his territories is as fair as it can possibly be. What they say makes clear that, with the division already made, asking his daughters to declare in public how much they love him is no more than vanity on Lear's part. Yet when Cordelia refuses to co-operate, he reveals she has always been his favourite and suggests that it is with her he intended to live. This issue of his future accommodation is a crucial one, especially as he wants to keep a retinue of 100 knights – no small number, even in a big castle, and one which will give to some of Goneril's later remarks a disturbing note of reasonable complaint. As the play progresses, she quickly emerges as villainous, if not *quite* so much as her sister Regan with her penchant for actually having an old man's eyes gouged out rather than simply suggesting it. Yet her initial remarks about the bad behaviour of her father's 100 knights seem to have some justification and the dilemma of a large household with two competing centres of authority would probably have been recognised at the time, and is perhaps still recognisable, as real. The trouble is that in transferring all his possessions to his two daughters, Lear cannot accept that he is also relinquishing his status and power. This is brought home to him by Goneril's servant Oswald after he has been challenged by Lear with the Jacobean equivalent of 'Do you know who I am?' Yes, insolently, but accurately, Oswald replies, 'My lady's father'. There is a vertiginous drop here from Lear's previous position in society, one that his Fool emphasises more cruelly when he is asked by the king why he is so full of songs. 'I have used it, nuncle,' he replies, 'e'er since thou mads't thy daughters thy mother; for [then] thou gav'st them the rod, and put'st down thine own breeches.'

In some ways (although by no means all!), *King Lear* is a domestic drama to which Shakespeare has given added intensity by having the action played out at the highest social level. The fate of the protagonist is not unlike that of the old landowner who features in a jest book published around the same time as the play was being performed.[3] He had made all his property over to his son who, in the beginning, found a place for his father at the top of the dining table. Gradually, however, he was moved down to the middle and the end before then being sent to eat with the servants. Finally, a couch was made for him behind a

---

3. *Pasquil's Jests* was published around 1604.

door where he died in grief and misery, covered with an old sackcloth. When his grandson is asked by his father why he wants to keep this sackcloth, he replies, 'Forsooth, it shall serve to cover you as it did my old grandfather.' Apart from this 'do-as-you-would-be-done-by' punchline (Elizabethan and Jacobean 'jests' are not always very funny), the progress of the old man is a lot like Lear's except that, because he is writing a play, Shakespeare has to accelerate it. The reduction of Lear's retinue of a hundred, for example, is not gradual but virtually instantaneous as Goneril and Regan subject him to a classic scissors' movement. Why do you need 25 knights, Goneril asks, or even ten or five, 'To follow in a house where twice so many / Have a command to tend you?', to which Regan adds, 'What need one?'

Accommodation, or living space, is often liable to be an issue between the generations. In Britain today it has taken what may be an unusual turn because parents who lived through a period when it was relatively easy to become a property owner find it is no longer possible for their children to buy a house, and therefore feel obliged to share living space with them in a way that is sometimes not especially comfortable for either party. The more familiar, historic situation is when parents have to live with their children because they have lost the power to look after themselves, are no longer strong enough, for example, to work the ground they own. There is a glimpse into this peasant world in *As You Like It* when the loyal old servant Adam is so appalled by the way the elder son of his former master is treating the younger that he offers Orlando the 500 crowns he has managed to save for his retirement, 'When service should in my old limbs lie lame / And unregarded age in corners thrown.' Like so many lines in Shakespeare, this last one has become almost proverbial. Its main force is no doubt metaphorical, but 'corners' also refers in a literal sense to how old people could be fitted in when only a small amount of room was available.

Neither Goneril and Regan, nor Adam's remark, encourage optimism about the prospects for a happy retirement in Elizabethan times. Shakespeare is not always so gloomy however. Launcelot Gobbo's opening address to the audience in *The Merchant of Venice* is interrupted by the entry onstage of a 'sand-blind' old man whom he recognises as his own father. The new arrival is looking for his son and Launcelot 'tries confusions' with him by not at first revealing that he is the very person of whom the old man is in search. This deception, depending on old Gobbo no longer being able to see much, appears to amuse Lancelot more than it usually does a modern audience but fortunately it is not lasting and before long he is kneeling down in front of his father and asking for his blessing. According to historians, this was a ritual that took place every morning in many Elizabethan households. Shakespeare presents it as a manifestation of warm family feeling, of the natural love that exists between parents and their children. In *King Lear* there is an emphasis on how *un*natural the behaviour of Goneril and Regan is. Lear himself tells Regan she must know 'the offices of nature, bond of childhood' and later compares 'filial ingratitude' to biting one's own hand for lifting food to it. He has nevertheless at least one daughter who understands what natural means in this context and Cordelia is the model for a number of future devoted daughters in literature.

A good example of one of Cordelia's literary descendants would be little Dorrit in Dickens' novel of that name. She is her often irritating father's faithful companion although, in other Dickens novels, caring for a parent is not limited to females. In chapter 25 of *Great Expectations*, for instance, the lawyer's clerk, Wemmick, invites the hero to his tiny house in the London suburbs and introduces him to his 'Agèd Parent', who is profoundly deaf. 'Nod away at him, Mr Pip, that's what he likes', Wemmick says, 'Nod away at him, if you please, like winking.' As Pip obliges, and so much so that he eventually becomes dizzy, Wemmick, who has developed a 'hard face' from his job as a bill collector in the City, visibly softens. He has hired a young girl to look after his 'Agèd P' in the daytime while he is at work and is clearly warmly attached to his father, however much that attachment may manifest itself in what strikes us today as an uncomfortable, and occasionally nauseous, degree of condescension.

Relations between young and old in the past, especially the more distant past, is not a topic about which it is easy to generalise. In the 1970s, the well-known cultural historian, Keith Thomas gave a crucial lecture to the British Academy on 'Age and Authority in Early Modern England'. This covered a great deal of ground, including the way those older people who had already secured commanding positions in particular organisations always tended to be keen on lengthening qualifying periods or apprenticeships so that any challenge to their own authority was delayed as long as possible. There are perhaps modern reflections of this habit in a relatively recent decision by the European Union that there should be no compulsory retirement age in universities. This was presumably to strike a blow against attitudes that were regarded as reprehensibly 'ageist', but it must have frustrated the younger generation and perhaps made them wonder where progress in their particular subjects was to come from. Yet, that young people should chafe against the restrictions imposed on them by their elders (although not necessarily betters) is familiar enough, and not perhaps any less 'natural' than the love that should exist between parents and their children. Giving up a privileged position an individual may have expended a great deal of effort and time to achieve is in any case not always easy and can lead to that unpleasant feeling of no longer having any clear social function, of being 'superannuated'. This is what Lear experiences as a consequence of the decision he himself has made to retire, and that he has not properly understood the implications of his voluntary change of status is clear from his fury as he realises his wishes no longer carry the weight they did. What is important, a counsellor at *Age Concern* might now have told him, is to have some other project to which he could devote his remaining time and energy, the 'crawl towards death' which he announces as his future intention, just before he makes a public distribution of his land, not being an especially good option.

After an interesting survey of what we would now call 'restrictive practices' in early modern England that hindered the young from progressing too rapidly – in seventeenth-century Oxford, Keith Thomas explains, it was seven years to the MA, fourteen to the BD and eighteen to the DD – only in the final part of his lecture does Thomas come to deal with how the old have been treated by society in the past. He is at that point chiefly concerned with questioning those 'modern sociologists' who have spoken 'nostalgically of the treatment of the aged in pre-industrial times' and talked of a period when an 'individual might anticipate old age with pleasure, as a time when declining physical energy would be compensated by social esteem for experience'. He quotes a leading gerontologist who describes how this 'Golden Age of living for older persons was disturbed and undermined by the Industrial Revolution' and then goes on to argue that any talk of a sudden change of this kind is fanciful. Having previously shown how patchy and inadequate pension arrangements were, even among the professional classes, he points out that for the labouring poor old age was as dire a prospect before as well as during the nineteenth century. Unless like Adam (who is a fictional character) an old person had money, or owned property, almost everything depended on having a supportive family. Yet, though children are the staff of old age, he quotes a seventeenth-century preacher as saying, 'God sometimes beats men with these staves instead of supporting them thereby.'

Reviewing Thomas' lecture, along with a book about *Growing Old in America*, Lawrence Stone decided its conclusion was inescapable and that 'in pre-modern England (and America) the old were respected only as long as they retained control of property'. He entitled his review, 'Walking over Grandma', a phrase from the boast of one of Richard

Nixon's associates that this was what he was cheerfully prepared to do in order to serve the President. As Stone points out, it illustrates that there has always been a strong inhibition against treating the old badly (who after all would walk over their grandmother?) but Lear cannot have been alone in discovering it is not one that can be relied upon entirely when other motives are in play.

The lesson of *King Lear* for those who contemplate retirement, or have it forced on them, is that things do not always work out too well. But Shakespeare's play was written a long time ago, and in social circumstances that were very different (we do not all have kingdoms to divide), so that perhaps equally relevant is an essay of Charles Lamb, published in *The London Magazine* in 1825. It is called 'The Superannuated Man' and describes the life of the kind of early nineteenth-century office worker that Lamb himself was for a long period. What it has meant is a waste of the narrator's 'golden years' since he began clerking at fourteen and then spent 36 more of them toiling away for six days a week, with only one free day at Easter and Christmas, and one week's holiday in the summer. This routine has brought him close to nervous collapse, worrying in the evenings whether he has made some significant clerical error, and had effects on his demeanour that his employers have noticed. When they call him to them, he believes it is because they want to give him the sack whereas, in fact, they have decided that, now he has reached 50, he can be allowed to retire on a pension worth two thirds of his normal pay.

This surprising turn of events means that the narrator is now 'superannuated' in the positive, rather than negative, sense of that word and Lamb is excellent at having him describe what this implies. He is like a long-term prisoner whose weak eyes are dazzled, on his release, by the unaccustomed light and, whereas in his one-week holidays he used to walk in the countryside for 30 miles a day, in order to make sure he made the most of his time off, he is now in a position where 'I no longer hunt after pleasure; I let it come to me.' He explains that, 'I have indeed lived nominally fifty years, but deduct out of them the hours which I have lived to other people, and not to myself, and you will find me still a young fellow.' There is a wry hint of complaint here but, in spite of any regrets he may harbour, he is fully determined to seize the opportunity that has been given him: 'My ten next years, if I stretch so far, will be as long as any preceding thirty.' This is the optimistic view of retirement that Lamb's narrator conceives above all in terms of escape from an occupation he has not enjoyed. 'A man can never have too much Time to himself', he says, 'nor too little to do'; and also, 'I walk about; not to and from.' Here, in these excellent words, is the unburdened existence to which Lear was looking forward and which he might possibly have enjoyed had he taken his decision to abdicate earlier, or managed his withdrawal more skilfully.

King Lear is widely regarded as one of Shakespeare's great tragedies, but it is reasonable to ask quite where the tragedy lies. Perhaps it is in the revelation of the depths to which human nature can sink that the division of Lear's kingdom reveals, the scant encouragement people need to prey on each other 'like monsters of the deep', as Albany puts it, one of the not especially effective forces for good in the play. It is Gloucester who is most inclined to place the cruelty that quickly begins to surface in the context of a disordered natural world, but then he is presented throughout as a superstitious man. If Lear himself is tragic it can hardly be because he qualifies as an Aristotelian great man, having behind him, like Macbeth, Othello or Antony, a successful military past. His sufferings are great although, had he been able to listen to Keith Thomas or Lawrence Stone, he would have been obliged to recognise that many of them are largely self-inflicted. In his book on 'constituting' old age in Elizabethan and early Jacobean England, Christopher Martin writes of the 'avid willingness' with which a power-hungry younger generation 'projects their own image of senescence onto the aged subjects' in *King Lear*, and how several of them are humiliated for 'trespassing the boundaries deemed suitable to their time of life'. His reading is a subtle and impressive one but tends to make Lear himself a virtually blameless *victim* of an ageist ideology and someone for whom we should therefore feel sorry. As so many theorists of tragedy have pointed out, victims are not tragic heroes, and what prevents Lear from seeming merely victimised (like Gloucester) is the force and intensity with which he protests against what has happened to him. 'I pray you, father,' Regan tells him, 'being weak, seem so' but it is a long time before he is ready to take her advice. 'Old age should burn and rave at close of day' enjoins Dylan Thomas in a frequently quoted poem, 'Rage, rage against the dying of the light', and no one rages more memorably than Lear.

Swift's Struldbruggs
Illustration by J.J. Grandville (1803-1847)
from the 1838 edition of *Gulliver's Travels*

3

Ageing, Decrepitude and the Wisdom of the Elders

Lear is clearly an old man but just how old is a problem for directors. There is a record of one production in which, when he first appears, he limps on stage supported by a doctor. This has the advantage of helping to explain his decision to retire, but it will seem incongruous in retrospect given the energy he displays in protesting against his misfortunes. Towards the end of the play, he does reveal that he is 'fourscore and upwards', which is usefully precise but might make one wonder (the case of Charlie Chaplin, who was a father very late in life, notwithstanding) why Cordelia is so often cast as a young woman. Her relationship with Lear can often seem like the particularly privileged one that sometimes develops between a grandparent and a grandchild, rather than that of a father and his daughter, more (that is) little Nell than little Dorrit; but then she may be the female Benjamin of the family, the child who coming last could, as the Bible suggests, tend to be favoured by the parents and therefore resented by older siblings.

As Thane's statistics make clear, there were far fewer individuals over 80, and indeed over 70, who were around in Shakespeare's time than there are now, which is why the idea of what then constituted old age must have been very different, and what was true of the Jacobean period applies to history in general, although there were always, of course, exceptions. Some of these are cited in Cicero's enormously influential and notably sanguine treatise on old age, which was written when he was in his early sixties but in which he adopts the persona of an 84-year-old Cato the Elder. It is Cicero who points out that Plato was 81, and still writing, when he died and that Sophocles, who is supposed to have lived until he was over 90, had to defend himself in court from an attempt by his sons to take over the management of his affairs, presumably on the grounds of senile incompetence, and did so by presenting the judges with his recently composed *Oedipus at Colonus*. Yet, in general, even taking into account how a high infant mortality rate can distort the life-expectancy statistics, the lifespan of individuals was much shorter in the past than it is now so that old age came quicker. 'That time of year thou mayst in me behold / When yellow leaves, or none, or few, do hang / Upon those boughs which shake against the cold,' Shakespeare writes in Sonnet 73 and he goes on to say that, 'In me thou see'st the glowing of such fire / That on the ashes of his youth doth lie'. No one knows quite when these words were written and the Sonnets are full of conventional poses that cannot be taken literally. It is evident, moreover, that, if the speaker feels that he is in the autumn or winter of his life, it is in comparison with a loved one who, in modern terms, could best be described as adolescent. It is, nevertheless, likely that, when Shakespeare retired to Stratford, he would have thought of himself as on his last lap, and that his death at 52 would not have been regarded as an especially early one. According to Maurice Charney, 50 was 'the conventional year for the onset of old age in men in Shakespeare's time' and the frame of reference this suggests is not so dissimilar to the one implied in Lamb's account of his superannuated man.

This relativity of the concept of old age is a topic that was discussed by Jean Améry, from several different points of view, in his *On Aging: Revolt and Resignation*. He was a philosopher who had many interesting things to say but who sometimes, like de Beauvoir, disappears into what, for some readers at least, will be the fog of the phenomenology or existentialism of his time. Yet he defines at least one feature of what he wants to call 'social age' plainly enough when he says that 'when Kennedy became president of the United States at the age of forty-three, he was young; a forty-three-year-old assistant university lecturer isn't'. In one section of his book he describes going to a lecture of Sartre's 20 years after having first heard him speak in public and having then had what was, at that time, his enthusiastic admiration for the man confirmed. What he says strikes him now more than a physical decline, which makes him fail to recognise immediately the virile and powerful figure he had first seen in the spring of 1946, is Sartre's social age by which he means, in this instance, that, for the crowds of young people who have come to hear him, he is already an established value so firmly anchored in the past that he cannot be part of any future they will enjoy. One consequence is, as Améry puts it, that the young people who emerge from the lecture, full of admiration and respect for Sartre, have in fact stolen his world from him in preparing to make it their own and that 'our social extinction at the point we become old is a foregone conclusion whether we are called Sartre or Mr X'. For him, this process of social ageing is worse than the biological variety; yet he paints such a vivid picture of Sartre's physical decline from the man he had known 20 years before that it is hard not to feel that, of all the many different ways of calculating age, biology still provides the one that is most secure. Sartre was already ill when Améry went this second time to listen to him and the effects of the ageing process are not in any case uniform; but the impression we often have that some people have suddenly become old, received a *coup de vieux* as the French say, is more often than not a consequence of our not having seen them for some time. Those with whom we live on a day-to-day basis age imperceptibly so that it takes an old photograph, or a sudden shaft of light as we are observing them (or ourselves in the mirror!), to bring home the truth that the years have indeed taken their toll.

The classic account of the difference that being away from people can make to how we perceive them comes towards the end of Proust's *Remembrance of Things Past* when the narrator, who has been for some years absent from Paris in a sanatorium, is invited to an afternoon concert at the house of the Duke and Duchess of Guermantes. On the way there he happens to meet his old acquaintance, the Baron Charlus, who has suffered a stroke and is reduced, according to his friend and carer, Jupien, to second childhood. Both his hair and beard have turned white so that the effect, the narrator claims, is to give Charlus all the 'Shakespearean majesty of a King Lear'. This majesty does not mean that, in the narrator's view, there are not visible consequences of the stroke which may be moral as well as physical. He draws this conclusion chiefly from the way that, when someone they both know passes by, the baron makes an elaborate greeting, taking off his hat and bowing as low as if the person concerned were the Queen of France. Since, in the past, Charlus has been a stickler for class distinctions, not to say a snob, and their mutual acquaintance would at that time have received no more from him than a nod, the narrator assumes that the changes age and illness have effected in him must have produced alterations inside as well as out. Yet what makes him unable to be quite sure of this is the thought that the elaborate nature of the old man's greeting might also be the consequence of the sheer physical demands of making any kind of gesture after his illness, and that these have caused him to exaggerate his movements.

This same doubt is less in evidence when Marcel, as Proust's narrator is called, arrives at the afternoon concert. His description of the de Guermantes' other guests has a comic verve worthy of Daumier. Most of them are unrecognisable at first sight and they all appear to be in fancy dress, or like well-known actors who have successfully disguised themselves as people much older than themselves. His one-time personal enemy, Monsieur d'Argencourt, for example, appears to have put on a flowing white beard and exchanged his previously proud and disdainful bearing for that of a trembling old beggar with an idiotic smile permanently fixed to his face. Marcel can just about recall the occasional smile tempering d'Argencourt's aloofness in the past but, even supposing similar intentions lay behind it now, 'the very substance of the eye through which he expressed the smile was so changed, because of the extraordinary transformation of his face, that the expression itself became quite different and even appeared to belong to a different person'. Given d'Argencourt's former unpleasantness, the ageing process in him might be said to have brought some advantages, and there are women at the concert whose faces are so altered that the narrator concludes that expressions of kindness and tenderness are now no longer impossible for them. To grow old, it seems, can sometimes ameliorate rather than degrade. However, we are given little indication as to whether or not this might be true of himself since, although there are so many striking details about changes in others – even those who have managed to retain their figures are described as looking like *withered* adolescents – there are none to indicate how he also might have become unrecognisable in old age, in spite of what he sees providing him with a mirror-image of his own condition.

In a close and interesting reading of this episode, Kathleen Woodward, whose psychoanalytical affiliations are made plain in the way the title of her book (*Aging and Its Discontents*) echoes that of a famous work by Freud, has called it a 'frightening hyperparable of aging in the twentieth century', and described the narrator as driven by vindictiveness to present a vision of old age that is 'hideous', a cruel vilification. What he cannot do, she suggests, is bring to consciousness 'the ideology associated with old age as decline' and as a result he is perpetuating, in his descriptions, 'a cycle of ageism'. That may or not be true but I doubt that these final scenes in Proust's book would have the currency they do were they not invested with a remarkable linguistic energy, which allows readers to put to one side the question that Woodward feels they should lead us to ask: 'Is it wise in personal terms to recognise oneself as old?' Wise or not, there are sometimes aching limbs that give an individual no choice and confirm that the decline age brings is not always or merely an ideology.

There are very many different manifestations of growing old but no instances of their complete absence. Old people who say they feel as young as ever could be said to be declaring their age in that a common characteristic of youth is not to listen to the body at all, and a similar point was being made by the biologist Lewis Wolpert when in 2011 he published a book, the subtitle of which was *The Surprising Nature of Getting Old*. The main title of this work was *You're Looking Very Well*, as if the unspoken accompaniment in addressing the elderly in that way is always 'considering'. Shakespeare gives his audience a visible indication of Lear's age by an explicit attribution to him of white hair and Proust's description of Charlus being like King Lear suggests this became common in productions of the play. The signal had been used by Shakespeare before at the end of *King Henry IV: Part 2* when Hal succeeds his father and dismisses Falstaff with, 'How ill white hairs become a fool and jester!'

Falstaff is perhaps the most celebrated example in English literature of someone who is determined to remain young, in spite of his white hair (and enormous bulk). As I have already implied, he constantly identifies himself as 'one of the boys', even if, according to Hal, he needs to unbutton himself after supper and goes to sleep on benches after noon. To the long list that the Lord Chief Justice provides of why he has no right to consider himself young, Shakespeare's Jaques in *As You Like It* might be said to make several additions, but then so also does Hamlet when he is asked by Polonius what he is reading. 'Slanders', he replies sarcastically, 'for the satirical rogue says here that old men have grey beards; that their faces are wrinkled; their eyes purging thick amber and plum-tree gum; and that they have a plentiful lack of wit, together with most weak hams.' What is significant here is that Polonius is the king's respected councillor and therefore a reminder that one of the supposed rewards of age, in compensation for the kind of physical disadvantages Hamlet lists, is wisdom, the wisdom of the elders. This is what Cicero sees as a major reward of old age, reminding his readers that one of the ruling bodies in Rome is called the Senate, a word derived from the Latin for an old man, and that, although old men may not be able to climb a ship's mast, he and his contemporaries are the best people to keep hold of the tiller. Wisdom is what Polonius dispenses to his son, Laertes, who is about to travel and is usually represented on the stage as bored to tears by his father's advice. The famous speech is indeed full of commonplaces ('Neither a borrower, nor a lender be' figuring as only one of them) and Polonius is on the whole seen by Shakespeare as very much the tedious old fool Hamlet calls him. With a tendency to forget what he is saying, and an inclination to wander off the point that irritates even the mild-mannered queen, he is inordinately fond of his own cunning (which turns out not to be so cunning after all) and has no qualms about spying on young people. Yet he is sufficiently self-aware to know that, whereas the young may lack discretion, the old often suspect more than they actually know; and his speech to his son would not have become so well-known if the commonplaces it contained were not also broadly true. Polonius is hardly the best advertisement there has been for the wisdom of old age but few spectators of *Hamlet* have ever concluded that he is thoroughly deserving of his sticky end.

Polonius is not the only 'wise old man' in Shakespeare; another is Nestor in *Troilus and Cressida*. He is memorably described by Thersites, who provides a cynical choric commentary on the action in that play, as 'old Nestor – whose wit was mouldy ere your grandsires had nails on their toes'. Yet, when Hector meets him, he says, 'Let me embrace thee, good old chronicle, / That hast so long walked hand in hand with time.' In calling Nestor a 'chronicle', Hector signals how, in many countries, the old have not only been respected for the advice they can offer, but also as living repositories of a particular society's laws and customs. This was especially the case where there were no written records and the main access to history was therefore through old people. Keith Thomas reports how dismayed the inhabitants of certain Oxfordshire villages were when an epidemic carried off the old folk 'so that there scarce remained alive any for upholding the customs and privileges of the parish' although this function clearly became less important the more a recording system was established, as well as when a society became subject to rapid change. Simone de Beauvoir argues in her book on old age that it was in part because Chinese society was so static for centuries that the old were able to play such a prominent role in it,[1] yet there have been other countries in Asia where they enjoy, and still do enjoy, great respect and influence. There is a highly simplified illustration of how important they must have been in traditional Japanese rural communities in Kurosawa's classic film, *Seven Samurai* (1954). Divided over how to deal with threats to their

---

1. *La Vieillesse.*

existence posed by local bandits who regularly steal their crops (and their women), the inhabitants of a village seek counsel from a person who is so visibly and spectacularly ancient, so 'blasted with antiquity' that he must be their oldest member. In a contribution to a collection entitled *Images of Aging: Cultural Representations of Later Life*, Shuichi Wada has argued that respect for the old was so deeply embedded in Japanese society, it managed to survive even the remarkable modernisation that followed the Second World War.

Someone with great faith in the wisdom of the elders is Lemuel Gulliver. In one of his conversations with Boswell, Dr Johnson observed how superior *The Tale of a Tub* was to all Swift's other work and said of *Gulliver's Travels*: 'When once you have thought of big men and little men, it is very easy to do all the rest.' He must sometimes have tired of Boswell asking him questions clearly designed to produce good copy and answered tongue-in-cheek. Whether or not this was what was happening here, his remark is patently unfair and it is anyway not only big and little men that Swift's imagination conjures up. In 'A Voyage to Luggnagg', Gulliver is excited to be told that, in the country he is visiting, children are very occasionally born with a mark on their foreheads that indicates they will live forever. The details are characteristically precise. This mark, Swift writes, begins as a red circular spot over the left eyebrow, turns green at twelve, deep blue at 25 and then coal black 20 years later, by which point it is 'as large as an English shilling'.

Gulliver feels 'inexpressible delight' at hearing this news. 'Happy nation', he says, 'where every child hath at least a chance for being immortal!' Amused by his naïve enthusiasm, his hosts ask how he would behave if he happened to be born a Struldbrugg, as these children are called. He replies that he would spend the first 200 years establishing a financial independence that resulted in his being 'the wealthiest man in the kingdom', while at the same time studying all the arts and sciences so that he was also its most well-informed member. By paying close attention to public affairs, he would become 'a living treasury of knowledge and wisdom' and no doubt therefore 'the oracle of the nation'. In this manner he would confirm what had been his initial impression on first hearing about the Struldbruggs, that it was a fortunate people which could have amongst it 'so many living examples of ancient virtue, and ... masters ready to instruct them in the wisdom of all former ages'.

Immortality begins to seem less of a boon, however, when Gulliver discovers that, although the Struldbruggs never die, they are not exempted from growing old. In one of the Greek myths, Aurora, the goddess of the dawn, falls in love with a young man called Tithonus and confers immortality on him, carelessly forgetting to ensure also that he does not grow old. In the 1830s Tennyson wrote a poem in which Tithonus laments being deprived of the human privilege of dying and complains, 'Me only cruel immortality / Consumes'. The effects of age are limited in Tennyson's description of Tithonus to white hair and withered feet but Swift is somewhat more graphic, explaining that, when they reach 90, the Struldbruggs lose their teeth and hair, eating or drinking whatever they can get, 'without relish or appetite. The diseases they were subject to, still continuing without increasing or diminishing.' The result is that, just like Tithonus, they learn to curse their own immortality and 'whenever they see a funeral, they lament and repine that others are gone to a harbour of rest, to which they themselves never can hope to arrive.' It might well be thought that Swift has cheated here a little by imagining a highly compromised form of living for ever. Yet, if he hadn't, he would still have been faced with a problem familiar to those who argue for the resurrection of the body. Just as it is difficult to imagine a soul freely choosing any particular stage of its body's physical development in which to live again, so it might have been hard for Swift to propose a precise moment or period when that development stopped and immortality kicked in. The solution he adopts is not entirely coherent, however, since it is hard to see how someone could continue to age while the illnesses from which they suffer neither increase nor diminish.

Growing old for ever is a gruesome prospect, as Swift makes clear and in ways one is tempted to say are also typical, different though they are from the early eighteenth-century realism of his description of the spot on the forehead. The Struldbruggs, Gulliver notes, 'were the most mortifying sight I ever beheld; and the women more horrible than the men'. No reason is given for this distinction. It is common now to defend Swift from the charge of misogyny but it is hard to know what other word fits his explanation that, should two Struldbruggs marry, their union is dissolved 'by the courtesy of the kingdom' when the younger of the two reaches 80: 'For the law thinks it a reasonable indulgence that those who are condemned without any fault of their own, to a perpetual continuance in the world, should not have their misery doubled by the load of a wife.'

Ageing is a natural process that does not only affect the body, as Swift was well aware. 'In talking', he writes, the Struldbruggs 'forget the common appellation of things, and the names of persons, even of those who are their nearest friends and relations.' This is an accurate description of what is called 'nominal aphasia', a technical term that sometimes invites the response from its sufferers, 'But my aphasia is not just nominal.' 'For the same reason', Swift continues, 'they can never amuse themselves with reading, because their memory will not serve to carry them from the beginning of a sentence to the end.' Here we are more obviously in the territory of dementia or Alzheimer's and the recognition of it certainly puts a damper on Gulliver's initial idea that, if he were a Struldbrugg, he would garner so much life experience that, along with a few others, he could form an 'immortal brotherhood' to guide and counsel society, giving 'perpetual warning and instruction to mankind'.

As I suggested, the more rapidly a society is subject to either industrial, cultural or technological change, the less the experience of the old will count. It is a rare computer expert who is still in demand at 70 and the call for a literary critic is not something that is now heard often along the corridors of a university English department. In D.H. Lawrence's *Women in Love*, there is a chapter in which he analyses with an acuity that can be surprising, given his popular reputation, the transition Gerald Crich effects when he takes over the running of the family mine from his father, whose style of management had been paternalistic. Trying to make a case for someone he feels has done rather well in the past but is now being laid off, the older man receives short shrift from his son:

> 'I've got a man in his place now, father. He'll be happier out of it, believe me. You think his allowance is plenty, don't you?'
>
> 'It is not the allowance he wants, poor man. He feels it very much, that he is superannuated. Says he had twenty more years of work in him yet.'
>
> 'Not of this kind of work I want. He doesn't understand.'

For those whose work involves physical labour, and whose joints begin to ache, retirement can often never come too soon. Lawrence's father was unusual in being able to work down the mine from the age of ten into his mid-sixties, a testimony to his good fortune, or to genes his gifted son was unlucky enough not to inherit. But for those whose occupation is largely sedentary or intellectual, there may be different forces in operation, one of which is being described here. The gist of the exchange must have been heard very many times since it was published, as firms and organisations 'restructured' and as early, or not so early, retirements ensued.

Lawrence is relatively neutral on the value of experience in his account of how the mines were re-organised, although he does say that the miners actually preferred a straightforward cash nexus to the complications of the old relationships with paternalistic employers. In the second of his *Four Quartets*, which carries the title of the English village from which some of his ancestors emigrated to America ('East Coker'), his contemporary T.S. Eliot is more forthright and reflects on the 'Long hoped for calm, the autumnal serenity / And the wisdom of age', which 'the quiet-voiced elders' had promised. Might the serenity they exhibit only be what he calls, in a notable phrase, 'a deliberate hebetude' and their supposed wisdom 'only the knowledge of dead secrets / Useless in the darkness into which they peered / Or from which they turned their eyes'? He points out that 'experience' is of very limited value since the pattern of events is never quite the same in the present as it was in the past and concludes:

> *... Do not let me hear*
> *Of the wisdom of old men, but rather of their folly,*
> *Their fear of fear and frenzy, their fear of possession,*
> *Of belonging to another, or to others, or to God.*
> *The only wisdom we can hope to acquire*
> *Is the wisdom of humility: humility is endless.*

Eliot is a poet who can startle his readers with the beauty of his language – just before these words there is a fine description of walking into East Coker at twilight, which ends, 'The dahlias sleep in the empty silence. / Wait for the early owl'. Yet, when he chooses to be ratiocinative, he can sound flat. Flatness is not so much the problem here as what quite he means in his description of the 'folly' of old men. Is the frenzy they fear their own or that of others and, if their 'fear of possession' is anxiety about relationships with other people as well as God, as the line that follows that expression would seem to suggest, why should it be more characteristic of the old than the young? These may sound like foolish questions but there appears to be in the verse private concerns that have not been made completely public. As for humility, although we certainly all need lots of that, the old may be said to have an advantage here given how often, as Proust's episode implies, it is commonly forced on them by nature. There is a famous French expression that is a variation on Eliot's point about the value of experience and which goes, *Si jeunesse savait, si vieillesse pouvait*, one way of translating which might be to say that you only begin to understand a situation when it is too late to do anything about it. Or, as a popular English saying more wittily, if less precisely puts it, 'Experience is the comb life gives you after you lose your hair.'

'Monkey Gland' Treatment
Advertisement for Serge Voronoff's book *The Conquest of Life*
from the *Chicago Tribune*, 1924

4

Self-consciousness and Sex

In the early 1960s a poet called Jenny Joseph wrote a relatively undistinguished poem called 'Warning', which somehow hit a nerve, became widely known and has lingered in the public consciousness ever since. Only 29 at the time, Joseph began her poem with, 'When I am an old woman I shall wear purple / With a red hat which doesn't go, and doesn't suit me'. Not having to worry about the impression her appearance makes on other people was not the only advantage the poet anticipated from the irresponsibilities of old age since Joseph talks also of looking forward to the day when she would 'run [her] stick along the public railings' and 'hoard pens and pencils and beermats'. The main emphasis, however, is on dress and the freedom she will have to wear a colour that is presumably regarded as problematic. Only recently, in an English provincial town, the opening lines of 'Warning' were displayed on the stairs leading up to an art exhibition organised around the colour purple.

The notion that in old age we can give up the struggle to look attractive or appealing to others is not entertained by every old person. For obvious reasons associated with the culture in which we live, or have lived for centuries, that imperative tends to bear down more heavily on women than men. 'Appearance is important to old people, not because we suppose it will impress other people,' writes Diana Athill in *Somewhere Towards the End*, 'but because of what we ourselves see when we look in the mirror'; but self-esteem of this kind is surely only a staging post in the search for esteem from others. The continuing need to look attractive is especially felt by women who are, or have been in the public eye, and probably helps to explain why former film stars like Greta Garbo and

Marlene Dietrich spent their old age in virtual reclusion. The rewards they can expect from keeping up the struggle are suggested by the gasps of amazement that accompany the appearance of stars such as Cher on television, even if the cosmetic surgery they may have undergone often means they can then only indicate their appreciation of the admiration focussed on them with a limited play of facial feature. On these occasions, it is customary for their interviewers to ignore the old convention about never asking a woman her age and for the audience, when it is given, to break into warm applause. This is strange when surviving into old age has very little to do with personal merit and is so largely a matter of good fortune; but it corresponds to the tradition, equally strange, that whoever manages to live to a hundred receives a telegram from the sovereign. 'If you can eat a boiled egg at 90,' Alan Bennett has somewhere said, 'they think you deserve a Nobel Prize.' One cannot help suspecting that those who applaud the 80 year-olds who are still able to talk coherently on television are thereby trying to ensure the same good fortune for themselves.

The dream of endless youth must have been around in Western culture since its beginnings but no amount of going to bed early, not drinking alcohol or avoiding stressful situations has yet allowed anyone to realise it. Oscar Wilde passed an ironic if incidental judgement on these matters in his *Picture of Dorian Gray*, the hero of which is a beautiful young man who has a portrait painted of himself when he is eighteen. His life thereafter is punctuated by episodes of meanness, debauchery and evil but his appearance does not change although his portrait, hidden away in a back room, becomes increasingly hideous. In the melodramatic finale, he stabs the painting and thereby both kills himself and takes on all the signs of ageing (and bad living!) it had accumulated. Although many of the procedures for attenuating these signs are new, they have behind them a long history of aids for keeping up appearances and disguising the effects of age. During the first half of the eighteenth century, Swift turned a jaundiced and unhealthy eye on what some of these then were as far as they concerned women. His poem 'A Beautiful Young Nymph Going to Bed' has an equally ironical subtitle, 'Written for the Honour of the Fair Sex', and gives a detailed inventory of everything an ageing prostitute has to take off or out before she tries to get some rest. This begins with artificial hair, a glass eye, and false eyebrows made from a 'mouse's hide'. Next come the 'plumpers' that have served to 'fill her hollow jaws' and, of course, a set of false teeth. Finally, there are the rags that have 'contrived to prop / Her flabby dugs', the 'steel-ribbed bodice; / Which by the operator's skill, / Press down the lumps, the hollows fill', and the padding for her hips.

As Swift's poem suggests, artificial aids for looking young are often not just a method for keeping up appearances but also for retaining sexual appeal and there is here another criterion for defining how old people are that can shift considerably over time. In general, the age at which women stop being regarded by the groups in which they circulate as sexually active beings, and accept to regard themselves in that same light, has gone up steadily; but how far up may sometimes have been associated with the social class to which they belonged. In his essay on Donald McGill, for example, George Orwell claimed that this artist's comic postcards reflected a 'working-class outlook which takes it as a matter of course that youth and adventure … end with marriage' and he went on to say that members of this same class 'age very much earlier' that those in the higher reaches. According to him, there was nothing biological or genetic about this phenomenon and nor could it be attributed to working men and women having such hard and difficult lives. The explanation lay rather in the willingness of the working class to accept the ageing process more easily than their privileged contemporaries. True though much of this might be of working-class culture, attitudes are usually related to economic circumstances (as Orwell well knew) and 'looking after oneself' calls for a certain degree of both means and leisure not always available to those on low incomes.

At times there may be a cult of youth that affects certain sections of society. In *As You Like It*, Jaques talks of the seven ages of man but in his period, and before, these were often described as three or four. As far as sex is concerned, the number can sometimes come down to only two: before and after real or potential sexual activity. This at least is what one might deduce from the 'superannuated belles and time-worn rakes' whom one critic (Elizabeth Mignon) once described as positively crowding the English stage between 1660 and 1700. For the authors of the Restoration comedies in which these characters appear, the line between the time when human beings are entitled to regard themselves as sexually active or available and that in which they need to recognise that they are no longer in the game, can be brutally drawn. The old or older man who still feels he can be attractive to a young girl is a stereotype that goes back to classical comedy and features in what must be hundreds of plays; somewhat less familiar is the older woman reluctant to throw in the towel, the superannuated belle of which the prime example in this period of drama is perhaps Congreve's Lady Wishfort in his *Way of the World*. When this character first appears, she is found in front of an array of cosmetics for resisting the ageing process that anticipate not so much Swift's 'Beautiful Young Nymph Going to Bed' as his more well-known 'The Lady's Dressing Room', in which there is a reference to Celia's 'ointments, daubs, and paints and creams'. Lady Wishfort needs aids like these because she feels that recent stressful events have left her looking 'absolutely decayed'. 'Your ladyship has frowned a little too rashly indeed, madam', her maid comments, 'There are some cracks discernible in the white varnish.' Her mistress responds by saying that she feels she looks like 'an old peeled wall'. Later in the play another character describes Lady Wishfort's forehead as wrinkled 'like a Coat of Cream-cheese', but the main judgement on her is that she has an 'old woman's appetite' (sexual is the word understood), which is depraved like 'the Green Sickness of a second childhood'.

The humiliation Lady Wishfort suffers in *The Way of the World*, and that which several like her undergo in other plays of the period, has the feel of a contemporary societal judgement, although one has always to remember that most of the authors of these plays were men and also perhaps that, ridiculous as she often is, Lady Wishfort is the main source of humour in *The Way of the World*, as well as (in my view) its most interesting and sympathetic character. She is in a long line of ageing females still interested in sex who testify to the strong misogynistic strain in British and, indeed, Western culture, and who are not always wholly defined by their intended dramatic context, or the more conscious intentions of their largely male creators. Rather than taking another example from eighteenth- or nineteenth-century literature to illustrate this point, it might be useful here to turn to popular culture and those relatively few female performers in the music hall who, denied the ability, for one reason or another, of basing their appeal on physical attraction, deliberately set out to be funny and were known in the trade as 'grotesques' (a technical term that tells its own story). Emerging from them into almost our time was a figure such as old Mother Riley, although 'she', of course, adds misogynistic insult to injury in being impersonated by a man in drag (as does 'Mrs Brown', one of her recent modern avatars). More, perhaps, to my point is a character who appeared regularly in the successful television sitcom, *Dinnerladies*, by Victoria Wood. A writer with a gift for the comic idiosyncrasies of Northern speech analogous to that of Alan Bennett, Wood was the sensible, shy central character called Brenda in this series. From time to time, she is plagued by sudden irruptions into the canteen where she works of her mother, played by the gifted comic actress Julie Walters. Calling herself Petula Gordino, she is a dishevelled, flatulent left-over figure from the hippy culture of the 1960s who lives in a caravan and continually borrows from her daughter to survive. The comic reversal at the heart of her conception is that, whereas Brenda has an extremely slow-burning and timid relationship with the canteen manager, her mother gives every appearance of being as sexually active in her old age as she was in her hippy youth, continually fantasising about the famous men who have been her lovers and at one point bursting into the canteen with her latest toy boy. Yet the part is so written that the comedy she creates is not entirely of a mocking, scornful variety with the result that, for all her selfishness and shameless exploitation of her daughter, Petula eventually becomes endearing.

The way sex in old women is treated clearly has a lot to do with who is writing as well as attitudes in society, or rather (in the case of Lady Wishfort) a particular sector of society of the time. Yet there can be special difficulties involved that have nothing to do with either. In a recent documentary about her life, Germaine Greer was asked whether she had ever bothered with hormone replacement treatment (HRT). She replied that she had been drawn to it in connection with an affair she had begun during her sixties and, with her characteristic frankness, explained that with age the vagina narrows and fails to secrete. HRT cannot stop this process, she went on, but it helps and at least makes an ageing woman penetrable. On the male side, what tends to diminish or fail completely is the ability to do the penetrating. In his *Psychopathology of Everyday Life*, Freud claims that Turks from Bosnia 'place a higher value on sexual enjoyment than on anything else, and in the event of sexual disorders they are plunged in a despair which contrasts strangely with their resignation towards the threat of death'. He recalls that a colleague had once described a Turkish patient of his having said to him, 'Herr, you must know that if *that* comes to an end then life is of no value.' Even though this is a view which may conveniently bolster Freud's own approach to the treatment of mental disorders, it can no doubt be assumed not to be limited to Bosnian Turks. Yet, as far as sexual activity brought to an end by advancing age is concerned, there is an opposing position that provides another of those contrasts found everywhere in the study of old age. According to Socrates, Sophocles was once asked whether he was still capable of enjoying a woman and was impressed when the great dramatist replied that he was glad to be free of all that business and felt that the disappearance of his libido was like an escape from being chained to a raging madman. Raging madman or not, what he seems to have been celebrating was the period when the sexual drive was no longer so preoccupying that it hindered him from taking a calm, rational view of the world.

For men, the perhaps even more successful equivalent of HRT is Viagra, which has behind it a long list of solutions and powders that bear as similar a relation to the modern drug as Swift's list of artificial aids does to today's cosmetic surgery. Someone who can easily be imagined as availing himself of all Viagra has to offer is Falstaff. In that scene from *King Henry IV: Part 2* to which I have already alluded in my introduction, the one in which Hal and his friend Poins disguise themselves as waiters so they can overhear the unflattering remarks that they are confident Falstaff will make about them, they are hidden observers of everything that passes between him and Doll Tearsheet. 'Is it not strange', Poins comments at one early moment, 'that desire should so many years outlive performance?' It was precisely this discrepancy which Viagra was introduced to rectify.

Another fictional character who attempts to overcome the disadvantages of age, but this time much more obviously in relation to sex than in Falstaff's case, is Baron Hulot in Balzac's great novel, *La Cousine Bette*. Balzac is not the most subtle of writers but he is particularly good at portraying people who are in the grip of an obsession or monomania. His Hulot had been a handsome ladykiller in the days of the first Napoleonic Empire but, when the novel opens, it is now the 1840s and he is having to rely on those aids to the preservation of youth that are not, and never have been, exclusively limited to women. Dying hair as it begins to go white, or replacing hair loss with a wig, as well as false teeth, are familiar enough but, when the action of the novel opens, Hulot is also opting for a corset to maintain his fine appearance – as did many corpulent individuals of his time (Balzac's fellow novelist Stendhal being one of them). His mistress in these opening episodes is a young woman called Josépha whom he has helped to launch on a career at the opera. Now that she has become successful, thanks in no small part to all the money Hulot has spent on her, she is in the process of finding another patron or, as we might say these days, sugar daddy, who is much richer than Hulot. He therefore decides to look for his next mistress among the young, dissatisfied wives of the lower middle class, rather than professional courtesans, and is lured into the orbit of Valérie Marneffe who is married to one on his subordinates at the War Office and initially sees an affair with the Baron as a way of securing for her husband a thoroughly undeserved promotion.

Valérie soon warms to her work and succeeds in so fascinating her husband's boss that he spends far more money on her than he had on his young singer, while at the same time she ingeniously strings along three other lovers. In his desperate determination to hang on to her, Baron

Hulot brings his family to the brink of financial ruin and threatens them all with disgrace by stealing from the government. His ever-advancing years do not lessen his addiction to sex and women and, after he has finally lost Valérie, his promise of reform proves to have no more validity than those of habitual, life-long drug-takers. Old and decrepit though he has become, he is able to acquire a series of very young, or, what we would think of now as child, mistresses because they, or their families, are poor enough to need the relatively small amounts of money he is still able to provide. In the final pages of the novel, after the death of his improbably saintly and long-suffering wife, he runs off with his family's kitchen maid, Agathe, who is at least 60 years his junior. It is a final grotesque tableau of January and May. As Balzac presents him, Hulot needs a young woman the way an alcoholic must have his next drink and nothing can stop him from seeking one out. The publishing conditions of the day, although far freer at the time than they were in Britain where Hulot's obsession could hardly have been depicted at all, do not allow Balzac to give enough graphic detail to confirm that the Baron is an example of desire outlasting performance, but that is what is strongly suggested. That is to say that what he is seeking to satisfy in his irresistible search may not be primarily a sexual need but a continuation of those psychological as well as physical triumphs he had enjoyed in his youth as an Empire *beau*. It is this idea of himself that age cannot force him, or many men in a similar position, to abandon.

In our time Baron Hulot would have gone to prison (or Thailand); but, had there been a trial, he could have cited a famous precedent in his favour. The Bible speaks of how when King David was growing old, and losing his body heat, his advisors went looking for a young virgin who could warm him up. Abishag, as the girl they found was unfortunately called, is thought by some commentators to have been no more than twelve and that her duties were not limited to warming is suggested by our being told David 'knew her not', a set phrase which does not so much indicate that the king exercised self-restraint than that even a young girl had not solved the problem of his impotence. The suggestion is not necessarily, however, that he was without desire or had cheerfully entered those calm waters which Socrates remembered Sophocles celebrating.

One criterion that has sometimes been evoked to mark the passage from young to old in women is the menopause. Rather less obviously marked in nature for men, the failure of the ability to copulate and therefore, by implication at least, to inseminate, has been linked by some of them to other, less physical aspects of creativity. Yeats is a poet who frequently declaimed against the encroachments of age and lamented the discrepancy between the continuing strength of his feelings and the body that was there to express them. In one of his most famous poems, 'Sailing to Byzantium', he characterised the old man he was then becoming, blind in one eye and increasingly deaf, as 'but a paltry thing, / A tattered coat upon a stick'. This is after having previously protested that a country where the young are in one another's arms could be no place for him.

It would be a brave commentator who offered to pin down the exact meaning of such an evocative and complicated poem as 'Sailing to Byzantium', but one of its suggestions seems to be the familiar one that the old can find compensation for physical decay in 'monuments of unageing intellect'. Yet, apart from the fact that most intellectual monuments are not, in fact, unageing, no less subject to damage or neglect than those in marble or stone, one is made to feel that this represents a choice Yeats would not have made had it not been forced upon him, if, that is, 'decrepit age' had not been, as he puts it in the second poem in *The Tower*, tied to him, 'As to a dog's tail'. In the last year of his life, he wrote that his imagination became 'stronger and stronger as this Foolish Body decays' and that by imagination he was not referring to anything exclusively spiritual is clear from his claim, in 'A Prayer for Old Age', that, 'He that sings a lasting song / Thinks in a marrow-bone'. In 'The Spur' he is more specific:

> *You think it horrible that lust and rage*
> *Should dance attention upon my old age;*
> *They were not such a plague when I was young;*
> *What else have I to spur me into song?*

If the poetic inspiration by which he set so great a store is as much a physical as spiritual matter, then it is difficult to see physical decay, and loss of sexual potency, as anything but a major misfortune. Balzac subscribed to the view that any emission of semen represented a diminution in his artistic creativity. The Goncourt brothers report how 'sperm was for him an emission of pure cerebral substance, a sort of filtering out and loss, through the penis, of a work of art' and describe how, 'after some misdemeanour or other, when he had neglected to apply his theory', he would turn up at a friend's house crying, 'I lost a book this morning!'[1]

---

1. This anecdote is recorded in Graham Robb's biography of Balzac.

For Yeats also potency and poetry were closely linked, or as Richard Ellman puts it in his biography *Yeats: The Man and the Mask*, 'Versemaking and lovemaking had always made connections in his mind.' This may be one of the reasons why, a few years before his death in his mid-seventies, he was happy to undergo what was known as the 'Steinach operation', a procedure that involved a partial vasectomy and promised rejuvenation. In the 1930s, this had begun to take precedence over the previous fashion for grafting tissue from monkey's testicles onto those of men. The 'monkey gland operation' as it was somewhat euphemistically known, and as it has been fully described in a book by David Hamilton, was very successfully publicised for its rejuvenating effects by a surgeon called Voronoff who was of Russian origin but based in France. In both instances, any positive results Voronoff and Steinach were thought to have achieved are now attributed to a placebo effect; but that in Yeats's case they wore off is suggested by 'Politics', the last poem in his final volume where he asks: 'How can I, that girl standing there, / My attention fix / On Roman or on Russian / Or on Spanish politics' and then exclaims, 'But O that I were young again / And held her in my arms.'

One further and evident problem with ageing which is relevant here is that it does not necessarily take place in a uniform fashion in all individuals so that, when it is a question of a relationship (as sex usually is), there is no inevitable synchronisation of what goes on in two different people. The pace at which they each reach what Lawrence called 'wrinkled ripe fulfilment' may vary considerably. In his *A Propos of Lady Chatterley's Lover*, he offers a utopian vision of a marriage in which this problem does not exist. Is there not, he asks, throughout the whole process of a couple's progress towards old age,

> some unseen, unknown interplay of balance, harmony, completion, like some soundless symphony which moves with a rhythm from phase to phase, so different, so very different in the various movements, and yet one symphony, made out of the soundless singing of two strange and incompatible lives, a man's and a woman's?

In the vague romanticism of these phrases there is perhaps the yearning wish-fulfilment of a man who, when he wrote *Lady Chatterley's Lover*, is widely accepted to have been impotent, or at least no longer sexually active, but whose wife Frieda, although six years older than he was, had by no means accepted that her own sex life was over. She continued to have affairs until his death, as well as after, and Lawrence's later fiction is full of complaints about women who, when they reach their fifties, are still full of vitality, and refuse to acknowledge that their sexual life is done. The problem for him was that, since meeting Frieda (and to some extent before), sex had been the cornerstone of his approach to life. As if aware of the possible difficulties this represents for his evocation of marriage as a soundless symphony, Lawrence follows it with a crucial qualification. 'But –', he writes, 'and this *but* crashes through the heart like a bullet – marriage is not marriage which is not basically and permanently phallic.' His only escape from looming contradiction here is through an interpretation of 'permanently phallic' as something far wider than sex as we normally understand it.

Lawrence's account of a harmonious married relationship comes in a section of *A Propos of Lady Chatterley's Lover* where marriage itself is being celebrated. This may well seem strange, given the novel he is defending deals with adultery, and Lawrence's popular reputation as the early twentieth century's most vehement advocate of sexual freedom is also hard to align with the implicit plea *A Propos* contains for (as the saying is) growing old gracefully. But then he is just one voice among many and attitudes to age and sex vary so much, as do individuals' experiences of them, that it would be impossible to generalise. Many Europeans still tend to think of the United States as a land of youthful energy and enterprise and might therefore be surprised that Americans have tended recently to opt for political leaders who are in their seventies. Perhaps this is related to the amount of money potential presidents are required to raise, or the way American political parties are organised since, if it was because the public actually valued experience and the wisdom of old age, candidates would have been advised to grow long white beards and stoop a little. In fact, of course, they make every effort to turn back the clock and look as youthful as possible, holding out the possibility to their supporters, perhaps, that they too do not have to decay and die. Yet that sex in old age can sometimes be a problem is nowhere hinted at more poignantly than in a short poem by Thomas Hardy, which is worth quoting in full – if only to justify what may seem like a mean description of Jessie Joseph's 'Warning', at the beginning of this chapter, as relatively undistinguished. To sound colloquial while at the same time sufficiently transcending ordinary language to qualify what one writes as poetry is a hugely difficult enterprise and one that, in the modern era, Philip Larkin has perhaps come closest to undertaking most successfully. Hardy's poem has no separate title and is therefore known by its opening line:

Self-consciousness and Sex

I look into my glass
And view my wasting skin,
And say, 'Would God it came to pass
My heart had shrunk as thin!'

For then, I, undistrest
By hearts grown cold to me,
Could lonely wait my endless rest
With equanimity.

But Time, to make me grieve,
Part steals, lets part abide;
And shakes this fragile frame at eve
With throbbings of noontide.

This poem is dealing with what a commentator on old age I shall talk about later (G. Stanley Hall) calls the 'terminal oscillations' which accompany the decline of the sex drive. It is hard to know how the subject could be more memorably expressed.

The Cumberland Beggar
Painting by William Bowness (1809-1867)

5

Family Matters

Old age has often been difficult to define, numerically speaking. Lear's 'fourscore and upwards' comes at the beginning of a period when, as Keith Thomas points out, individuals were only just beginning to acquire a clear notion of exactly how old they were. The previous but also continuing absence of that notion probably explains why, in one London parish alone, the burials of no less than twelve centenarians were recorded between 1583 and 1599 or why, when a man called Harold Jenkins died in 1670, he was assumed to have been 169.[1] Sceptical as one might reasonably be about these figures, there is no doubt that some very old people did exist in former times, even if they were far less numerous than they are today, and one person who appears to have been especially attuned to noticing them was William Wordsworth. He spent a remarkable amount of time in his twenties and thirties travelling around the country on foot, often alone but sometimes with a male companion or his sister Dorothy. This was partly because he had so little money but, as he tramped the roads, he must have come across people much poorer and less fortunate than himself: abandoned women, discharged soldiers but also old men who had no family to support them and had slipped through the gaps of the distinctly patchy and inadequate welfare systems of the time.

That there were such systems is evident from Wordsworth's poem describing 'The Old Cumberland Beggar', first published in the second edition of *Lyrical Ballads* (1800). Its narrator, who has recently returned to his native regions, claims that he remembers this figure from his own

---

1. The details are in Thomas' lecture.

childhood when he already appeared so old that he scarcely seems any older now. He survives chiefly by visiting various village houses at set times during the week and begging from their far from rich occupants what are usually small items of food. There are those, we learn, who would like to see old men like the Cumberland Beggar housed by the authorities, just as today they are people who would discourage the public from giving money to the homeless on the streets because it only extends the period before they decide to take up the beds which are often (although not always) available and seek help for their addictions or psychological and other problems. The narrator is hostile to this approach. 'May never House, misnamed of Industry, / Make him a captive', he says and feels that the beggar serves a useful social purpose by inciting the locals to charitable acts and allowing them to feel better about themselves afterwards. Seeing him every week helps to prevent that hardening of the heart which results from never being challenged by the sight of fellow human beings in distress. Let the Beggar's blood, he declares, continue to: 'Struggle with frosty air and winter snows; / And let the chartered wind that sweeps the heath / Beat his grey locks against his withered face.'

The old Cumberland Beggar is closely observed. At the beginning of the poem, he is described as sitting down on a low stone structure used for getting on and off horses and looking through the scraps of food he has managed to collect 'with a fixed and serious look / Of idle computation' (perhaps a version of T.S. Eliot's 'deliberate hebetude'). As his 'palsied hand' lifts some of this food to his mouth, all his efforts cannot prevent crumbs being scattered everywhere; but the birds that are gathered round do not yet begin to peck at them because they are too close to where he is sitting. It is a vivid picture. Birds also feature in a description of an old man, published in the first edition of *Lyrical Ballads* and usually called 'Old Man Travelling'; but there they have become so inured to his presence that they 'regard him not' while he himself is 'by nature led / To peace so perfect, that the young behold / With envy, what the old man hardly feels'. 'Animal Tranquillity and Decay' was an alternative title chosen for this sketch and its idea seems to be of the decaying body slowly and painlessly merging back into nature. Bizarre as it may seem, the person Wordsworth could be remembering here is Rousseau who, in his *Discourse on Inequality*, talks of how, in a state of nature, the appetite of old people conveniently diminishes along with their means to satisfy it and claims that, being free of those diseases society brings, they exit this world without anyone much noticing, and almost without noticing themselves. Old soldiers never die, as the old song goes, they only fade away.

The revolutionary originality of Rousseau was to conceive of civil society as largely a *decline* from a state of nature, rather than the advance it had always been assumed to be in the writings of most previous political thinkers and in those of Hobbes, in particular. As a young man, Wordsworth was a political firebrand and a great admirer of Rousseau so that what might seem paradoxical is how the idea of old people being absorbed back into nature might lead into attitudes which strike us now as unsympathetic, not to say reactionary. He does not enquire, for example, how the old Cumberland beggar himself might feel about the wind beating his grey locks against his withered face, and there are no details in that poem about where he sleeps at night. In this period, the most obvious option would be the poor- or workhouse but that would mean accepting certain rules and restrictions, just as today rough sleepers who seek shelter indoors from one of the charities have to follow at least a minimum of regulation. In Wordsworth's time obligatory labour was the rule for those still capable of it, hence 'House of Industry'; yet it is not a libertarian objection that he makes against the beggar being swept up in the current welfare system, but that he would not then be able to fulfil his function as a stimulus to charitable feelings in others. There is an argument that paying taxes – and in Wordsworth's time there was a Poor Law levy – so that the State can look after those less fortunate than ourselves too conveniently insulates us against what might be the uncomfortable proximity of human distress; but, in making the case for local charity, Wordsworth treats the beggar as a cog in a wheel and gives the impression of not being at all interested in him as a fellow human being.

Different in every way from 'The Old Cumberland Beggar' in its treatment of old age is a poem from the first edition of *Lyrical Ballads* called 'Simon Lee: The Old Huntsman'. Whereas 'The Old Cumberland Beggar' and 'Old Man Travelling' are in a blank verse that allows for all kinds of subtleties, this is in the jingling ballad form which sometimes produces effects that teeter on the ludicrous and were meat and drink to those contemporary critics who were contemptuous of Wordsworth's 'simplicity'. The paradox is that it is in this poem, rather than the other two, that he is most realistic about the physical problems that can afflict old age. Simon has been an enthusiastic huntsman for his employers, blowing his bugle and running so fast in front of or alongside their horses that sometimes, 'He reeled, and was stone-blind.' Now that the local manor house is empty, the years have caught up with him so that, in addition to having lost an eye:

> *He is lean and he is sick,*
> *His little body's half awry,*
> *His ankles they are swoln and thick*
> *His legs are thin and dry.*[2]

His only remaining resource is a small patch of poor land close to his house that he and his wife are too weak to cultivate effectively. The more he labours the more – and it was this kind of detail the critics I refer to dwelt on – 'His poor old ancles swell'. The narrator comes across him as he is struggling to cut through the stump of an old tree and is able to lend a hand by severing it with one blow. Simon is effusive in his thanks and the poem ends with four lines that demonstrate that a degree of subtlety can be achieved in the ballad form after all:

> *I've heard of hearts unkind, kind deeds*
> *With coldness still returning;*
> *Alas! the gratitude of men*
> *Has oftener left me mourning.*

In an essay on 'Wordsworth and the Question of Ageing', which appeared in a special number of the journal *Romanticism* in 2019, Mark Sandy dispensed with any unease that might still be created in a reader by the ballad form of 'Simon Lee' by claiming that the poem was 'seriocomic' and that the effect of its mixed tragic and comic tones was that its protagonist is presented to us 'with empathy and disdain, delight and derision'. The narrator's removal of the stump, he went on, is an 'ill-judged act of kindness that renders Simon's existence bereft of purpose':

> Futile as Simon's daily struggle was, his tussle with the decayed tree trunk symbolised his one last lingering attachment to life and the living. Metaphorically, the uprooting of the tree 'stump' signifies Simon's final detachment from life and community. The narrator's action both short-circuits the possibilities of wider sympathies Wordsworth's ballad seeks to elicit and

---

2. As given in the 1798 edition of *Lyrical Ballads*. Later publications vary slightly in their wording.

positions Simon (now left in a state barely recognizable as living) beyond the communal fellowship of others.

This is not how I read the conclusion of Wordsworth's poem and nor can I find in it any evidence that his attitude to its subject is either disdainful or derisive.

The most obvious way for the old to avoid the 'House of Industry' and its equivalents, or the hit and miss of private charity, was always to be looked after by their children; but, although Simon Lee is married, he is childless, while the decayed and supposedly tranquil old man of Wordsworth's sketch is travelling to a hospital in Falmouth where his sailor son is already dying. The advantage of a family is not only that its members might be there to look after parents as they grow older, but also that it can satisfy what Hannah Arendt calls, in an essay on 'The Concept of History', the '"common man's" natural yearning for deathlessness'. It is aspects of this second idea that Wordsworth explores in what is by far his most impressive treatment of old age, the long narrative poem in blank verse which he somewhat pointedly (given its grim content) described as a 'pastoral' and called by the name of its principal character, 'Michael'. Michael is a version of Shakespeare's Adam in *As You Like It* in that he remains fit and healthy in extreme old age. He has, we learn at the beginning of the poem, a 'bodily frame [that] had been from youth to age / Of an unusual strength', words that are repeated at its end, but with ironic effect. The owner of an isolated sheep farm in the Lake District, he and his wife Isabel live a life of incessant labour but, like Abraham and Sarah in the Bible, they have been blessed with a son after the usual time for child-bearing has passed (when, that is, he is about 60 and his wife 20 years younger). The birth of Luke has transformed their lives. As Wordsworth puts it, with a psychological insight with which he is too rarely credited:

> ... *a child, more than all other gifts*
> *That earth can offer to declining man,*
> *Brings hope with it, and forward-looking thoughts,*
> *And stirrings of inquietude, when they*
> *By tendency of nature needs must fail.*

Having a son gives meaning to the life of labour Michael and his wife lead since they now have someone to whom they can hand on their farm after they are gone; but in that fine phrase 'stirrings of inquietude', Wordsworth indicates that it also gives them something to worry about and saves them from the apathy that old age so often brings.

Michael has spent half his life freeing his property from debt but, when his son is eighteen, he is unexpectedly called on to repay a loan that he had guaranteed for his once prosperous brother. The choice that faces him is either to sell off some of his land or to send Luke to a relative in town where he can earn some money. Loth as he is to part with his son, who for several years has been helping him to look after his sheep and to whom he has always been devoted, he decides on this latter course, principally so that his property can remain intact. Before they part, he asks Luke to help him lay the cornerstone of a new sheepfold, which the farm needs, but which will also serve as an emblem of their life together. The hopes Michael and Isobel pin on their son are disappointed and, once in town, he goes to the bad or, as Wordsworth puts it, gives himself 'to evil courses'. The despair this engenders is indicated in the poem by a description of how Michael afterwards often went to the sheepfold he had meant to build but 'never lifted up a single stone'. As in 'The Ruined Cottage', Wordsworth's other great tale of rural tragedy, the remnants of human striving persist in Nature as a symbol of how often it is frustrated.

It is not because Michael worries that, in the event of his wife's death, there will be no one to look after him that he mourns the alienation of his son, although that is in any case a burden which traditionally falls (Wemmick notwithstanding) more on female than male offspring. They are the ones who tend to be more crucially involved in that unofficial contract previously mentioned whereby children look after their parents in exchange for the care they have received before they could look after themselves. What hardly needs saying is that it does not always work. There may be no children, they may have died prematurely, or they may fail to respond appropriately like Lear's two daughters; or like those of 'Father Goriot' in Balzac's version of the Lear theme to which he gave that name. They are not quite heartless monsters like Goneril and Regan but, having reduced their father to miserable poverty by squandering all the money he has willingly and lovingly handed over to them, are too preoccupied with their own affairs to attend his funeral. What, however, perhaps needs to be said about this talk of a contract, is that it is distinctly lopsided. There is, after all, usually an element of choice in having children – at certain periods parents have deliberately had as many as possible in order to insure themselves for the future – whereas no one can choose to be born. Moreover, it is reasonable to believe that there is a duty of care which can stretch well beyond helpless infancy, and which is sometimes so neglected that children can feel any obligations they may have once incurred should be cancelled out. As John Locke, that expert on social contracts, puts it, 'the honour due from a child, places in the parents a perpetual right to respect, reverence, support and compliance too, more or less, as the father's care, cost, and kindness in his education, has been more or less'. Futile as it is to speculate beyond the bounds provided by *King Lear*, the way Goneril and Regan feel able to judge their father, who has 'ever but slenderly known himself', does not suggest that they owe him too much gratitude for their upbringing, or that he would ever have had the time or temperament to fulfil his parental duties adequately.

    Yet a pattern of reciprocity has mostly always been, and to some extent still is, normal, and nor is Wemmick the only example of a male offspring fully acknowledging its implications. He is a fictional character but Alan Bennett, for example, has written well in several different non-fictional forms about the difficulties of looking after his mother as her dementia worsened, without ever suggesting that he would be prepared to ignore what he instinctively felt was his duty. His accounts of visiting her in hospitals where she is surrounded by other women who have similarly lost their minds can be very funny (dementia being naturally profuse in those non-sequiturs which are often the mainstay of certain kinds of comedy) but, at the same time, they are touching and at no point does he give the impression of wanting to abandon his parent, or that he would feel justified in doing so. The portrait of the old father in David Lodge's *Deaf Sentence* may be part of a novel but he has made it clear that it is based on his own parent's increasing loss of mental control and it suggests very much the same decent attitudes as Bennett's.

    It remains the case, however, that it is daughters rather than sons who are more usually involved in looking after their old parents and no surprise therefore that, in the work of perhaps Wordsworth's most distinguished female contemporary, relations between daughters and (in her case) fathers, figure prominently. When one thinks of daughter/father relationships in Jane Austen, the case that is likely to come first to mind is Elizabeth Bennet's in *Pride and Prejudice*. Faced with a silly wife and a bevy of daughters, only two of whom he considers to be rational creatures, her father has retreated into ironic detachment and fallen into the bad habit of treating most of the world around him (apart from Elizabeth and her elder sister) as a comic spectacle. The catastrophe that overtakes his family when a young army officer runs away with one of his girls is clearly attributed by Austen, at least in part, to his failure to fulfil his role in the family contract, to a lapse of parental responsibility.

The example is not an especially relevant one, however, because Mr Bennet never seems particularly old. More pertinent to my theme are the main characters in Jane Austen's *Emma*.

The father of Emma Woodhouse is an example of the paradox that, whereas old people have fewer and fewer years in front of them and ought therefore to feel, when danger threatens, that they have much less to lose than the young, they often grow more timid as their strength diminishes. Mr Woodhouse's hypochondriac anxieties are such that they once led a critic to consider him the finest argument for euthanasia in English literature.[3] Yet in spite of her egotism in her treatment of her protégée Harriet Smith, Emma fulfils what she thinks of as her filial duties to him without ever complaining. She is the ideal carer so that the only threat on Mr Woodhouse's horizon is that his daughter should marry. What is never mentioned, or even hinted at, is that Emma might end up like many young women of the time and sacrifice her own marital prospects for the sake of a parent; but there is no danger of that when her chief and obvious, if undeclared, suitor turns out to be a man whose notions of what a child owes to her father, or indeed a father-in-law, are at least as traditional as her own. Of course, it makes a huge difference that Jane Austen is not dealing here with the rural poor, like Wordsworth, but with a section of English society where there is plenty of money available so that Mr Woodhouse can look forward to at least as much cossetting after Emma's marriage as he has enjoyed before it. The finale is therefore a happy one, for him, and for the reader, as Emma is safely united with a man who has been felt to be the appropriate partner for her all along.

This provision of happy endings has no doubt something to do with Austen's continuing and enormous popularity but she would not be such a good novelist if she did not make us aware of other possible scenarios, in the precarious situation of Jane Fairfax, for example, or even in Miss Bates, the ageing single lady who is the victim of Emma's heedless wit and who is represented as keeping up a shabby genteel existence on a very small income. In her book on old age in women writers, Devoney Looser criticises Austen for presenting Miss Bates as the kind of stereotypical spinster described in the three volumes of William Hayley's *Philosophical, Historical, and Moral Essay on Old Maids* (1785). Yet rather than indicating an inability to think beyond stereotypes, the treatment of her suggests to me a painful alertness in her creator as to what the fate of someone like herself could eventually

---

3. F.R. Leavis, in conversation, puckishly.

be without the emotional and, above all perhaps, financial support of a prosperous family.

Austen's final completed novel also has a happy ending but there the indications of unpleasant alternatives are much stronger. The heroine of *Persuasion*, Anne Elliot, has a younger sister already married and an elder one considered by most people better looking than herself. Since she has failed to find herself a husband and is widely thought to have 'lost her looks', it seems very much as though she will be condemned to staying at home and looking after her widowed father. This would not matter so much if he were a harmless, well-off fusspot like Mr Woodhouse, but Sir Walter Elliot is in fact a monster of egotism and vanity, not so much a candidate for euthanasia as patricide. So preoccupied with his good looks that he disapproves of the navy as a profession because of the effect sea air has on the complexion, Sir Walter judges everyone he meets by their physical appearance. Austen describes him with an incisiveness that sometimes makes him seem like a Gillray or Rowlandson caricature of an ageing rake (except that the stigmata of ageing are hardly apparent in his case), an early English version of Baron Hulot, but without the sex. There are, however, as always in Jane Austen, faint hints of sexuality, on this occasion in the way Sir Walter's pride in his personal appearance makes him vulnerable to the intrigues and advances of a widow, much younger than himself. The understated significance of these is that a second marriage would be likely to have serious financial implications for Anne, leaving her after her father's death much less comfortable than she might have been. Of course, no such marriage happens and Anne Elliot is saved in *Persuasion* by the reappearance of a former suitor who has been newly enriched by his time in the navy and who is able to restore to Anne her previous 'bloom'. The obligations she might have otherwise felt towards her father are ones which, being a dutiful daughter, she would have fulfilled, had she remained unmarried; but in that case they would have constituted, in the struggle between the generations often brought about by ageing, a cruel and blatant oppression of the old upon the young.

There are myriad variations on how relations between children and their ageing parents develop and one of the problems of relying on literature is that it tends to deal with only the more exceptional or unusual examples. Yet statistical tables are scarcely more informative, or informative in a quite different way. As a coda to the theme of fathers and daughters, it is perhaps helpful to look at that brilliant novella, or short novel, by Henry James called *Washington Square*. The immediate link here is that the central male character, Dr Sloper, is such an obvious fictional descendant of Mr Bennet in *Pride and Prejudice*. A successful New York physician, Sloper has lost a beautiful and clever wife as well as a son to sickness and is left alone with a daughter called Catherine whom he thinks plain and not especially bright. Partly because he finds it hard to hide his disappointment in her, and is so much cleverer than she is, he almost never addresses Catherine (James writes) 'save in the ironical form'. When a handsome and smart young man turns up and begins to pay court to her, he recognises at once that Morris Townsend, as the young man is called, must only be after her money.

At first, Dr Sloper is 'more than anything else amused with the whole situation', but then he takes steps to defuse it by making clear to Townsend that, should he marry Catherine, he would have access to the $10,000 a year her mother has left her, but nothing at all from him. Since he is a rich man, the difference is considerable and eventually leads Townsend to conclude, falsely as it happens, that he could do better with his fortune-hunting elsewhere. The trouble is that meanwhile Catherine has fallen deeply in love and is heartbroken when he eventually abandons her. No one could say that Sloper was not right to protect his daughter from a man like Townsend, who would not only have taken her money but also almost certainly made her unhappy; yet the methods he adopts show no insight into her feelings, and very little sympathy for them either. One of the perennial problems in literature is how to distinguish irony from sarcasm. James offers to perform that task for his readers after Townsend has made it clear to Catherine that he will not marry her, now he is sure her father will never change his mind about her inheritance. When Dr Sloper cannot resist coming to his daughter in order to enjoy the pleasures of 'I told you so', she makes a feeble pretence of having herself broken off her engagement to which her father then responds with, 'You are rather cruel, after encouraging him and playing with him for so long.' In the simplest of its definitions, irony is saying the opposite of what you mean, or what you know to be the truth. Dr Sloper is perfectly aware that it is Townsend who has been cruel and playing Catherine along. His remark is described by James as the doctor's 'revenge' but that thereafter Catherine refuses to reveal to him how 'deeply and incurably wounded' she has been by the episode is called his punishment for 'the abuse of *sarcasm* in his relations with this daughter' (my italics). This usage would appear to confirm that there is, in fact, very little difference between irony and sarcasm, with the second no more than a stronger, although perhaps also cruder version of the first.

Catherine has always admired and loved her father and, as he ages, she is never anything less than loyal in looking after him, but something is broken between them. After hearing that Townsend is once again back in New York, and feeling that he may not now have long to live, Dr Sloper asks Catherine to promise that, once he is dead, she will not consider marrying her former suitor. His daughter's own method for exacting revenge is to refuse to give that undertaking, even though she has no intention of taking up with Townsend again and, after her father's death, does in fact send him curtly away when he tries to re-establish the relationship. Her gesture is not an especially dramatic one, not of the order (for example) of the refusal of his dying mother's request that he should pray which haunts Stephen Dedalus in Joyce's *Ulysses*, but it does also demonstrate one of the many ways in which the need the old sometimes feel to be certain of knowing what will happen after their death can be frustrated.

Ramesses II
Statue from the 'Ramesseum' at Thebes

6

Leaving One's Mark

As Wordsworth's story of Michael makes clear, children are not always the most reliable route to making one's mark in the world and ensuring some kind of continuing presence in the future. This is especially the case if you only have one. Some time ago, one of the weekend newspapers ran a feature about a man who, on a conservative estimate, had fathered over 200 children. Mildly autistic, he could not imagine himself ever being married and so became a donor to various sperm banks, calculating that, as he grew older, at least some of the resulting offspring would want to get in touch and quieten his anxieties as to 'Who will remember me when I am gone? Who will talk about me? Who will be my heir?', and other such questions he described as keeping him awake at night. In the event, a small number of his progeny were curious enough to want to discover their biological father and one or two of them eventually established relations with him. 'The pharaohs built pyramids', he was reported as saying, 'These children are my pyramids.'[1]

His remark is a reminder that, instead of or in addition to children, rich and powerful individuals have in the past often sought to ensure a post-mortem future for themselves by overseeing the design and construction of tombs and mausoleums – although anyone who has ever visited a provincial French cemetery, and seen the rows upon rows of great slabs of concrete or marble that constitute the local family vaults, will know that this form of post-mortem commemoration can stretch well down the social scale. It is an impulse that Robert Browning

---

1. The weekend newspaper was the Saturday *Guardian* for 24 November 2018.

satirised in his dramatic monologue, 'The Bishop Orders His Tomb at Saint Praxed's Church'. Gathering members of his family around his death bed, including at least one son, the sixteenth-century Catholic bishop in question is feverishly concerned that his tomb should be made of the best materials and thereby outshine that of an ecclesiastical rival, 'Old Gandolf', who has stolen a march on him by dying first and securing a niche in Saint Praxed (a real church in Rome) that the bishop had been eyeing for himself. He wants the best inscriptions and the most elaborate decorations: 'The Saviour at his sermon on the mount', together with Pan, 'Ready to twitch the Nymph's last garment off'. Buried in his vineyard, he says, is a large lump of lapis lazuli with which, like those pharaohs concerned to take some of their material possessions into the afterlife with them, he wants to be buried. But he is worried that his relatives will ignore his wishes and keep for themselves the money he intends for his monument. Then he would be deprived of the satisfaction of old Gandolf having to look across Saint Praxed's at the new tomb with envy, just as in the past he envied the bishop his young mistress. These are, of course, Renaissance churchmen in Rome and, for Browning, Catholic dogma does not prevent them having feelings about how their lives will proceed after death, which have nothing to do with heaven and hell, any more than it prevents them from having children.

A serious variation on what Browning is mocking can be found in all the chantry chapels that were built in pre-Reformation Britain. The provision made in wills for these would also include money for the maintenance of a priest or two whose job it was to say prayers for the deceased, and especially those souls who would be presumed to have to make their way through Purgatory. The belief was that, by this method, the passage to a happier state could be accelerated or eased. The rationale for these buildings was therefore strictly theological (as perhaps it was also for the pyramids) but it is hard not to see both as also answering that anxiety as to 'Who will talk about me?' which the sperm donor expresses. When the English Church was reformed, the notion of Purgatory fell out of favour, news which somehow failed to reach Hamlet and his father but which had previously helped to allow Henry VIII (and his immediate successor) to expropriate or sell off the considerable wealth that chantry chapels had by their time come to represent. Yet what they illustrate here is that people who try to make provision for some kind of continuing presence after their deaths tend to do so on the assumption that the political and social conditions with which they are familiar will not change. The relatively sudden disappearance of the concept of Purgatory from the corridors of power, if not the psychology of the British nation, is one striking example of how often they do.

If even in Nature nothing lasts *for ever*, how much more true must that be of human affairs. The pharaohs could be said to have done well by their pyramids in that they at least cause us to remember them; but it seems that not every pharaoh had one. Ramesses II was one of Egypt's most successful and long-reigning kings but by the time he came to the throne, pyramid building appears to have gone out of fashion. He did, however, build a temple for his future corpse and had huge carved statues of himself erected all over his kingdom. It is one of these that Shelley reports having heard about in his sonnet known by the Greek version of Ramesses II's name, 'Ozymandias'. The narrator in this well-known poem describes having met a traveller from 'an antique land' who in the desert has come across two huge legs of stone which were 'trunkless'. Lying nearby, half sunk in the sand, was the statue's head with enough features still visible to indicate a frown, a 'wrinkled lip, and sneer of cold command'. On its still surviving pedestal were the words, 'My name is Ozymandias, king of kings: / Look on my works, ye Mighty, and despair!' There was of course no one in the flat desert landscape surrounding the 'colossal wreck' to be impressed.

Shelley was a radical, which is why he was so angry with Wordsworth for having moved from what, in the politics of the 1790s, was the extreme Left to being a crusty old Tory. His poem is a protest against authoritarian rulers such as Ozymandias but it may be also that it carries the hidden implication that art will always trump power. Whether it does or not, this is the belief that Shakespeare states explicitly at the beginning of his Sonnet 55:

> *Not marble nor the gilded monuments*
> *Of princes, shall outlive this pow'rful rhyme;*

As all the commentaries indicate, the assertion made here had been made very many times before, and it would often be made subsequently: political power is one thing but, in temporal terms, it can often prove inferior to poetry and the power of the word. One of those who makes this claim is Gibbon, but in a surprising way. 'The romance of *Tom Jones*', he writes in the introduction to his autobiography, 'will outlive the palace of the Escorial, and the imperial eagle of the house of Austria.' One might have expected him to have cited here a classical author, or even to have suggested that, although empires may decline, accounts of how they did so may well live on, so that it seems to me to alter any estimation of his character in a favourable direction to find him referring to the enduring fame of a comic novel.

Shakespeare talks of his verse surviving into the future but it is hard to see much evidence of his having any great concern for his own literary legacy, a body of work that would keep his name and memory alive once he was gone. Studying as he clearly did his contemporaries, he must have known that he was more gifted than any of them; but, in those last years spent mainly at Stratford, there are no indications of an anxiety to preserve all he had ever written, or anticipate those former colleagues from his acting company who would be responsible for a collected edition of his work in 1623. While certain members of the class from which he drew his patrons were studying plans for their monuments, he seems to have enjoyed enough financial and even critical success (his plays were popular) not to have been too concerned by what we know as posterity. That the bust which his widow eventually had placed in his local church made him look, in the memorable words of one critic, like 'a self-satisfied pork butcher'[2] was not something over which he had any control; but, had he been overly concerned about these matters, he could easily have made appropriate arrangements before he died.

The critical success Shelley enjoyed was negligible, which must have been galling, especially when the writing of his close friend Byron had made him an international celebrity. But then he was probably too young when he drowned to have been much troubled by the hope that the world would come to recognise how valuable his work actually was after his death. Someone who did nourish this hope as he became older, and was forced to recognise the mediocrity of any immediate success he had enjoyed in the literary world, was his French admirer and contemporary, Stendhal. When he resigned his commission in the French army and set out to be a writer, Stendhal exhibited a degree of self-belief similar to the one that allowed Wordsworth to withstand all the pressure from his relatives to 'get a proper job' and the scornful contempt that came from some quarters on the publication of *Lyrical Ballads*. What the young Stendhal wanted, he himself wrote in his literary journal, was 'to acquire the reputation of the greatest of French poets, not through intrigue like Voltaire but through true merit'. He decided that his way of doing this would be with the composition of comedies like Molière's.

The problem with this project was that, when Stendhal actually began to compose plays, he found he was incapable of writing verse (a rhyming couplet could take him over three hours of painful labour to complete).

---

2. John Dover Wilson.

What would eventually come to his rescue was a change in the cultural climate that led to drama in verse falling out of fashion. Byron's great European success was based on narrative poems but it was preceded and then succeeded by the equal, if not greater, triumphs of Walter Scott who, after beginning as a poet, turned to telling his stories in prose. As the nineteenth century advanced, and thanks partly to Scott, the novel increasingly became the dominant literary form with effects on those who might be concerned about their likely literary legacy similar although antithetical – strange as the analogy might seem – to those that the fading away of the concept of Purgatory brought about for whoever had left provision in their wills for chantry chapels. That is to say, a radical change in social and cultural circumstances led, on the one hand, to those who had pinned their hopes on chantries having more or less wasted their money whilst, on the other, a quite different change dispensed those in search of literary fame from being able to write verse. Stendhal was one of those who couldn't but then he could write prose and published three novels in his lifetime, two of which (*The Red and the Black* and *The Charterhouse of Parma*) are now regarded as masterpieces. That was far from being a widespread view in his time and, as he whiled away his later years as a French consul in the then dreary Italian port of Civitavecchia, troubled by all kinds of illnesses, he came to accept and believe that he would have to rely on posterity to decide just how talented he was. He took care to have his many unpublished writings copied and bound, entrusted them in his will to a loyal cousin and predicted that it would only be in 1880 that his work would be properly appreciated. That this prediction proved to be uncannily accurate is an encouragement for all those who hope that their literary legacy will outlast 'gilded monuments', although, if the rise of the novel could be said to have been a major factor in keeping Stendhal's memory alive, there may come a time when, with the increasing dominance of the visual media, prose is as little read as poetry is now, and Stendhal will be completely forgotten. Even today, whereas in the 1960s and 1970s what helped to keep his name alive was the way *The Red and Black* seemed to chime with feelings about social mobility dramatised in novels such as John Braine's *Room at the Top*, it may often be necessary to explain who he was.

Educated towards the end of the eighteenth century, Stendhal was an authentic child of the Enlightenment and had no discernible religious faith. There is therefore something uncharacteristically irrational in his reliance on posterity, the comfort he drew from a future fame he would never be around to enjoy. Those responsible for the construction and maintenance of chantry chapels were acting in a manner that was perfectly logical within the system of beliefs they espoused; but for those for whom any kind of personal afterlife is a myth, it makes little sense to imagine a belated celebrity. One of this century's philosophers coined the term 'post-mortem sentience'[3] for what is so memorably expressed by Claudio in Shakespeare's *Measure for Measure*:

> *Ay, but to die, and go we know not where;*
> *To lie in cold obstruction and to rot;*
> *This sensible warm motion to become*
> *A kneaded clod; ...*

If we can project our feelings forward in order to imagine what it would be like rotting away in the grave, so also (it would seem) can we look ahead to a moment when our previously neglected merits will be finally recognised. In his *Leviathan*, Thomas Hobbes recognised this peculiarity of human psychology and took the trouble to define it (using 'posterity' in a different sense from the one that has been adopted here):

> And though after death, there is no sense of the praise given us on Earth ... yet is not such Fame vain; because men have a present delight therein, from the foresight of it, and of the benefit that may rebound thereby to their posterity: which though they now see not, yet they imagine; and any thing that is pleasure in the sense, the same also is pleasure in the imagination.

Max Beerbohm was sceptical about what Hobbes describes (how can anyone be sure that the 'present delight' they take in their future fame is not a delusion?) and went to the trouble of satirising it in a short story about a minor poet of the 1890s whom he called Enoch Soames. Frustrated by his lack of success and convinced (like Stendhal) that the value of his work would one day be recognised, Soames sells his soul to the devil for the privilege of being transported to the British Museum 50 years into the future so that he can read all the appreciative references to his work that he is convinced he will by then be sure of finding there. Yet all he discovers is a footnote with a brief reference to him in a book on the 1890s by Max Beerbohm. The history of English literature is, nevertheless, full of writers the value of whose work was unrecognised

---

3. The philosopher was Frank Cioffi. There is a brilliant if somewhat ghoulish evocation of various aspects of post-mortem sentience in Leopold Bloom's reflections at the funeral of 'poor Dignam' in Joyce's *Ulysses*.

while they were living and who came to be appreciated after, sometimes long after, their deaths. Their cases offer hope to those who, coming to the end of a long writing career, are forced to acknowledge that they have made little or no impression on their contemporaries. Yet to derive satisfaction from what we can never know and never experience (will the climate-challenged world even exist in a hundred years' time?) is very strange, despite what the usually hard-headed Hobbes has to say about its validity.

According to Freud (and others), human beings find it difficult, if not impossible, to imagine themselves dead. One of the pastimes in which old people indulge is to organise their own funerals. There is a lot of sense in this since it takes the conditional out of that all too familiar phrase, 'This is what they would have wanted'; and it also relieves the surviving relatives of the burden of choosing the music, texts to be read or even talks, now habitually called 'eulogies' (which does not provide their givers with much room for manoeuvre). What is hard is for any old person to take on this task without imagining that he or she will be there, as a secret onlooker. This is the dream explicitly entertained in that popular music hall song, 'Ain't it grand to be bloomin' well dead', in which the singer is watching all his friends and relatives as they file past at his funeral. 'Some people there were praying for my soul', he sings, 'I said "It's the first time I've been off the dole"'; and then also, '"Spend the insurance", I murmured, "for alack / You know I shan't be with you going back."'

Maria Edgeworth's first published novel was called *Castle Rackrent* and satirises the extravagance, alcoholism and irresponsibility of late eighteenth-century Irish landlords in an unusually lively and burlesque fashion (she herself having the care of an estate in Ireland, along with her father). The story is told by a faithful old retainer in a particular property who describes how the last in the line of the family that owns it, and before the accumulation of debts leads to its being finally taken from him, decides he would like to be present at his own funeral, or more pertinently, in this Irish context, at his own wake. Whereas in funerals the emphasis is supposed to be on mourning those who have died, in wakes it falls more on celebrating how they have lived (as well as on the participants' relief in still being alive). In Liverpool, the old joke goes, the difference between a wedding and a wake is only one fewer drunk. Sir Condy, as the proprietor who is in the process of losing his estate is called, feigns death so that a wake can go on around him but then, when the bedclothes prevent him from hearing clearly what is said, stages a rapid resurrection and decides to join the party. 'But to my mind', the narrator observes 'Sir Condy was rather upon the sad order in the midst of it all, not finding there had been such a great talk about himself after his death as he had always expected to hear.'

Writers who rely on posterity to recall their passage in this world and to ensure that their presence here could be said to have had some meaning, beyond whatever is provided by a family, or any donations attached to their name which they may have left, reveal an implicit desire to know what will be said about them, not so much at their funerals but in the years afterwards. Someone who found an ingenious, if very limited, way of satisfying these feelings was Bruce Frederick Cummings. He confesses that his 'infant mind was bitter with those who insisted on regarding [him] as a normal child and not as a prodigy'. At a time when natural science was in high repute, his first ambition was to become an eminent zoologist and he overcame the disadvantages of a modest social background to land a job at London's Natural History Museum. Then, as this seemed more and more like a dead end, he turned to his second childhood ambition, which was to become a great writer, following in the footsteps of H.G. Wells, who had also begun as a zoologist. Before he could progress far along this route, he was diagnosed with multiple sclerosis and therefore had to pin his hopes for future celebrity on a journal in which he took his own frustration at not being likely to live long enough to fulfil his ambitions as a principal subject, inspecting himself with 'ruthless candour', as he says, and just as he might a specimen in the laboratory where he worked.

The title of this work Cummings laboured over was *The Journal of a Disappointed Man* and he gave himself the pen name of W.N.P. Barbellion. It is dominated by the idea of his death coming as an ignominious anti-climax, after all he wanted to do, and felt himself capable of doing. 'What more perfect', he writes, 'than the death of Rupert Brooke at Syros in the Aegon', and he thinks in contrast of that old man Wordsworth 'rotting at Rydal Mount'. His reference is to the fact that, after having studied a number of old men, Wordsworth himself became one, dying just after his eightieth birthday in his house in the Lake District, the qualities that had made him such an exciting and original poet in his youth having deserted him so that very little of what he wrote in the second half of his long life has any value. The stereotype of the literary geniuses who, as it were, live so intensely that they 'burn themselves out', which Cummings is relying on in his allusion to Brooke, has therefore nothing to do with Wordsworth, or indeed Coleridge, but is rather associated with the so-called second generation of romantic poets: Byron who died of what might well have been malaria when he was 36; Shelley who drowned when he was barely 30 and, of course, Keats who, like Cummings, was a victim of disease and only survived to his 26th year. Keats is in fact one of Cummings' heroes and some of the nature descriptions in his journal have an almost parodic Keatsean flavour. Of a field full of green grass, for example, he writes, 'every stalk was so full of sap ... that it would have bled great green drops' and, observing a rowing boat making slow progress, he notes that 'the water came off the languid paddles in syrupy clots'.

Cummings is a much better writer when he exploits his misfortunes by anatomising them and demonstrates that fearing the worst is no guarantee against the worst happening. What torments him is that, while his work at the museum has become drained of interest, his efforts to make an impression in the literary world, with time fast running out, are almost fruitless also. His agonised feeling that, without his journal, there would soon be no evidence of his ever having existed, meant that, like Stendhal, but even more so, he took extravagant care for the safety of the manuscripts from which the published version of his diary would be selected. Housing them in a specially made box when the outbreak of the First World War brought the possibility of bombing raids, he also attached a notice to the top of this box offering a guinea to anyone who saved its contents from damage by fire. When his selected version was published in March 1919, its last lines are two entries from 1917 that read 'October 14 to 17: Miserable' and 'October 21: Self-disgust'. There is then a 'Finis' followed by 'Barbellion died on December 31'. Since Cummings survived into October 1919, two years later and six months after his book's publication, this fiction not only allowed him to observe how his work was received by the critics but also estimate more accurately than would have been otherwise possible, what his chances of post-mortem fame were likely to be. He would have read the comments of reviewers as if, like the singer in the popular song, he was able to observe the guests at his own funeral.

The case of Cummings does not fit very well into this context because, for him, the ageing process was accelerated by a cruel disease and he died young. What nevertheless gives it some relevance is that one problem of life might always seem to be what we ought to do with what is still left of it, and he could also be said to offer an interesting device whereby those old people with literary ambitions can check on whether they have left their mark on the world (even though it is not one which could tell Cummings himself how long the mark would be visible). Without enough money to have a monument built or, more modestly perhaps, some kind of structure that could be called after him ('the

Cummings room'), writing was the only means he had of trying to live on into the future. He could think this way because, in his day, being a published writer carried with it a good deal of social prestige. With the triumph of the visual media, that is much less so today and neither was it always the case in the past. Ian Hamilton's excellent account of how the works of great writers were treated after their deaths in his *Keepers of the Flame: Literary Estates and the Rise of Biography* begins by recalling a description of the last days of John Donne that Izaak Walton had given in 1639. Desperately ill and emaciated, Donne forced himself to get out of bed and stand upright, dressed only in a winding sheet, while a life-size effigy of him was carved in wood. This was because, Walton remarks, a wish for self-perpetuation is surely 'rooted in the very nature of man'. That his writings could be a means to that self-perpetuation does not seem to have occurred to Donne. He may well have hoped his sermons would be preserved but, as a reformed character with a wild youth and now the Dean of St Paul's Cathedral, he seems not to have wanted to draw attention to his *Songs and Sonnets*. As Hamilton makes clear, it was almost by accident that these marvellous poems survived so that they could emerge into the limelight in the late nineteenth century and then become a part of my own, and that of so many other young people's, growing up in the years after the Second World War.

Writers sometimes claim that what they produce is only for themselves and it is true that their activities are ones which can satisfy certain very private psychological needs. Yet nearly all composition is addressed to someone, somewhere, even if that someone inhabits the future. In order to protect themselves from the charge of egotism and guard against libelling the living, it was the custom in the past for autobiographers to insist that whatever they wrote should only be published after they were dead, which was Wordsworth's stipulation for *The Prelude* (the autobiographical poem he kept working on into his old age but very rarely improved). When more obscure individuals write their memoirs without any prospect of publication in the usual sense, then or later, and many do, they often insist it is 'for the children'. It may well be so, and the children concerned may be grateful to have a written record of aspects of their parents' lives they would not otherwise know; but in the writer him- or herself there is likely to be also the need make sure that their passage through life has not gone unrecognised.

One of the most elemental and apparently primitive manifestations of the urge to make one's mark in a way that will be lasting comes in the environmentally damaging practice of carving initials on the rocks or trees of any famous tourist site people happen to be visiting. We are inclined to associate this habit with those of low intelligence. Yet, when Shelley and Byron visited the Château de Chillon, that imposing castle at the eastern end of Lake Geneva, part of the foundations of which are in the water, and which has dungeons impressive enough to have prompted Byron to write a long poem about what it would be like to be imprisoned in them, both poets scratched their names on one of its pillars, declaring as they did so a future temperamental affinity with even the ubiquitous and mythical Kilroy. What they wanted to indicate was that they had been there too. Not to take leave of this world without some indication that one was once here appears to be a strong feeling of many people in all walks of life, not just the poor and uneducated. As Henning Mankell, the Swedish writer best known in Britain as the creator of a detective called Wallander, has said in a book written when he was dying: 'Everybody I know has at some point carved their name onto a tree in the woods or scratched their signature onto a cliff by the sea. Nobody wants to be forgotten. But nearly everybody is.'[4]

---

4. From *Quicksand: What it Means to Be a Human Being*. This book corresponds in some ways to Enright's *Injury Time*.

Reading the Will
Painting by David Wilkie (1785-1841)

7

Will Power

As I have suggested, the decline in Lear's status until he is no more than 'my lady's father' is also a loss of power. Whereas before his abdication he had only to speak to get things done, he now has nothing to back up his demands apart from the persistence of old habits and whatever feelings of loyalty and respect he has previously managed to inspire (in the Earl of Kent, for example). Power drains away from him quickly, as it is said to do whenever a British prime minister makes the mistake of announcing a future retirement date. At a lower social level, the loss of power with the onset of old age is purely physical, as Wordsworth shows, not in his 'Michael' but in his 'Simon Lee'. Yet, in social contexts where physical strength is not the chief criterion, the power that is lost is much more dependent not only on rank but also material possessions, so that the way these are to be disposed of on the death of their owners can become a weapon not only for controlling certain aspects of the future but also for what happens while they are still alive.

Writers have understood this so well that a last will and testament frequently occurs as a plot device in their work. An unusual, early example here is Ben Jonson's *Volpone*. First staged about the same time as *King Lear*, and by Shakespeare's own company, this play gave Jacobean audiences the opportunity of realising how lucky they were to have two great playwrights who could never be mistaken for each other. Jonson's starting point is a confidence trick devised and implemented by a not-so-young *magnifico* of Venice, whose name gives the title to the play, and his quick-witted valet or 'parasite', Mosca. Volpone is a rich man with no family and, by pretending to be at death's door, he attracts a number of unsavoury characters who bring him generous gifts, hoping in this way to be written into his will as its chief beneficiary. Thanks to the ingenious lies Mosca tells them, they regard these presents as investments they will soon recover, especially as Volpone does such a convincing imitation of coughing and spluttering his way to the grave, while Mosca applies to his master's eyes an ointment which makes them ooze that 'thick amber and plumtree gum' mentioned by Hamlet. The three marks or gulls taken in by this trick are all given the name of birds, Voltore, 'the vulture', Corbaccio, 'the raven' and Corvino, 'the crow'. The most interesting of them, in this context, is Corbaccio. This is because he is as old as, if not older than, Volpone and ferociously consumed with the idea of both outliving him and inheriting all his valuables and money.

Jonson earned a well-deserved reputation as a 'classical' writer, someone who drew his inspiration from Greek and Latin authors, and his Corbaccio is the traditional old man or *senex* from classical comedy. One of the character traits regularly attributed to this figure is avarice. This is initially surprising since one might think that the older one becomes, the less conscious one would be of needing money, just as the fearfulness also often associated with this figure can (as I have said) seem strange when he, or perhaps she, has so many fewer years to lose than a young person. On closer inspection, the courage of young people may be because their bodies have not yet taught them what it might be to suffer, while old people's fondness for money might be attributed to their feeling that, as the light begins to fade, there is nothing more certain to hang on to. It is not an amiable trait but it is notable that in literature, for each old man who seeks to give away his possessions before he dies (as Lear does), there are ten determined to hang on to them.

When the play begins, Volpone has a memorable speech in which he worships at the shrine of his treasure house but, as the action progresses, it becomes clear that he derives less pleasure from his accumulation of precious objects than from deceiving people, a pleasure so intense that it will eventually lead to his downfall. There is no such division within the character of Corbaccio, who is so anxious to get his hands on these objects that he allows himself to be convinced by Mosca into disinheriting his son and leaving all his own property to the supposedly dying Volpone. This is child's play for a Mosca who, when his master takes a fancy to the beautiful young wife of another of the gulls, explains to her insanely jealous husband, Corvino, how the doctors have decided that Volpone is at a stage where the only thing that can help him is to lie in bed next to a young woman, 'lusty and full of juice', and then convinces him to offer this own wife for this service. This is all so he can become Volpone's sole heir, which is also Corbaccio's hope and belief. Of course, Corvino mistakenly thinks that Volpone is in such a moribund state that he will be incapable of 'knowing' his wife (to use the word from the obvious Biblical precedent), and Corbaccio calculates that, because he is certain to outlive Volpone, he will eventually be able to leave his son all the richer. Both are willing to take these extreme measures because they find the temptation of Volpone's wealth irresistible.

Volpone ends happily, with the bad characters punished and the good ones rewarded, so that it is therefore, according to the simplest of all the definitions, a comedy. Less certain is quite how *comic* it is or was meant to be. 'No laughing matter' is how one critic once described the plays of Jonson, who, in his notebooks, claimed that Aristotle was right to say that 'the moving of laughter is a fault in comedy, a kind of turpitude, that depraves some part of man's nature without a disease'.[1] Yet the scene in which Corbaccio first appears is clearly comic and meant to provoke laughter, or at least a smile. Of all the physical disabilities of old age, two chief ones are so common that they hardly rated a mention in my second chapter. Rare are those who, as they grow older, do not find that their eyesight or hearing deteriorates. Despite that scene between Lancelot Gobbo and his father in *The Merchant of* Venice which I have already mentioned, blindness or partial sightedness is not usually considered a joke. There are, nevertheless, other examples of lack of vision being used on the stage and on screen for comic effect, even in modern times. A popular cartoon figure of the period after the Second World War, for example, was Mr Magoo whose comic misfortunes were almost entirely based on the fact that he could hardly see; and, when Peter Cook opened a branch of the Establishment Club in New York, he began by saying that he was blind and using an excellent system called Broile before adding, 'I'm sorry, I'll feel that again.' Perhaps these examples say more about why Hobbes was not so wide of the mark when he tried to define what makes us laugh than our attitudes to old age.

Not being able to see properly, or at all, can be made comic but, in general, it is a disability that usually incites sympathy and inhibits laughter. Deafness on the other hand, as David Lodge has complained in *Deaf Sentence*, a novel in which the main character is rapidly losing his hearing, 'is always comic'. What it allows for on the stage are those comic misunderstandings which stretch from Jonson to the music hall and beyond. As Mosca tries to convince Corbaccio, in that first scene in which he appears, that Volpone's health is drastically deteriorating, the old man seizes on the wrong word, not having heard the rest, and

---

1. The critic was Neville Coghill (I believe).

has to be reassured that in fact the invalid is getting much worse. 'No amends' is the answer Mosca gives to Corbaccio's first enquiry as to how his masters is faring, but the deaf old man interprets this, with alarm, as indicating that Volpone is on the mend so that Mosca has to insist – 'loudly' is the stage direction – that this is not, in fact, the case. His words reassure Corbaccio and make him less insistent that the opiate he has brought with him should be given by Mosca to Volpone, purportedly to help the sick man sleep but no doubt to finish him off. Those who seek to exert power over the people in their immediate environment by dangling before them the benefits of their own death will run the danger, if not of positively encouraging others to bring that event about, then at least of ensuring that it will hardly be greeted with unalloyed sadness when it does happen.

Having assets to dispose of confers power on the old but can also incite complicated feelings in potential beneficiaries. Many writers, and particularly novelists, have been alert to the dramatic possibilities this creates. In Dickens's *Martin Chuzzlewit*, for example, old Martin as he is known (the novel is called after his grandson of the same name) is aware that many of his relatives are looking forward to profiting from his death. He has therefore taken the precaution of hiring a young orphan girl called Mary Graham to look after him, on the clear understanding that, although she will be well provided for while he lives, there will be nothing for her after he is gone. This method for making sure that there is at least someone who is happier to see him alive than dead is however threatened when his grandson falls in love with Mary and wants to marry her. His response to young Martin's refusal to give her up is to disinherit him.

It is because his expectations have been disappointed that Martin becomes an apprentice architect to Mr Pecksniff, who later will be one of the unpleasant people circling around old Martin's money, and then sails to America in a vain attempt to make his fortune. When he comes back no richer than when he left, matters are sorted out in a typically satisfactory and Dickensian manner, with no one of any merit disappointed. As in all Dickens' novels the narrative is complicated but there is an important subplot relevant to my theme in this chapter that involves old Martin's brother, Anthony. He is also rich and has a son called Jonas whom he has brought up to have the same grasping, avaricious attitude as himself, and who is therefore anxious for his ailing father to die. Jonas certainly intends to murder his father and, until chapter 51, both he and the novel's readers are led to believe that he has done so; but then it is revealed that the old man had discovered his son's plot against him and died rather of a broken heart. Before his death he had heard a voice, which told him that the intended crime 'began when I taught him to be too covetous of what I have to leave, and made the expectation of it his great business'.

Although Dickens creates all the conditions for patricide, it could be argued that there is a Victorian squeamishness in him that shies away from representing it. There are no such inhibitions in Émile Zola but then, in writing his grim tale of peasant life called *Earth* or *La Terre*, he was working in a different culture and, more importantly, dealing with a quite different tranche of society. He could well have been aware also of what was said about a certain kind of old man in a history of the French peasantry published in 1874 and sometimes cited in accounts of this novel:

> He carries the wretchedness of his last days with him from cottage to cottage, unwelcome, ill-received, a burden to everybody and to himself, a stranger in his children's house. At last he dies … but it is well for him to make haste, for greed is there, and greed nerves the arm of the hidden patricide.[2]

Such things are no longer possible in this country, one might think, where a 'peasant class' did not survive as long as it did in France. Nevertheless, the record indicates they once were and (as I make clear in my introduction) they suggest problems of which there are at least faint echoes today. Nothing strikes me as more reasonable, for instance, than that people should petition for what would be an eminently sensible change in the law which would allow assisted suicide. This would put an end to the horror of needless suffering in those who are certain to die anyway, protect from prosecution people who accede to a desperate partner's plea to help him or her end a life in cases where no hope is possible, and take away the unfairness of a final trip to Zurich only being available to those who can afford it. Yet opposition to the change does not only come from a largely Catholic minority for whom all life, in whatever tortured or damaged form it persists, is God-given and sacred. In addition to the pressures which might be brought to bear on old people to sign the forms that legalise their own assisted suicide, because they feel themselves a burden to their relatives, and the psychological instability of those in acute pain, there is also the problem that answering a family member's desperate appeal to help him or her die can become especially hard when doing so would bring a financial advantage.

---

2. The historian who studied the French peasantry was called Eugène Bonnemère and is quoted by de Beauvoir in her book on old age.

For French and English peasants, it was land which tended to provide a point of conflict between the young and the old whereas, for the business class Dickens often depicts, it is money in a more general sense. On occasions, there are also other factors that can be shown playing a similar role. In 1882, Anthony Trollope, one of Dickens' more important rivals and successors, published a short novel called *The Fixed Period*. This dealt with an imaginary island colony close to New Zealand where, following its independence from Britain, the new government has passed a law stipulating that, a year before each of its inhabitants reaches 67½ (more or less Trollope's age at the time of writing), he or she will be removed to a special 'college' to be looked after very comfortably before then being disposed of in a painless manner. The narrator is very proud of this innovation, pointing out that it would both protect the island's population from all the misery and pain of ageing while at the same time saving it a great deal of money. Moreover, he suggests that this wholly rational extension to what was in Trollope's time a lively debate on eugenics would prove a valuable innovation in humanitarian as well as economic terms:

> It would keep us out of debt, make for us our railways, render all our rivers navigable, construct our bridges, and leave us shortly the richest people on God's earth! And this would be effected by a measure doing more good to the aged than to any other class of the community!

The satirical intention of *The Fixed Period* is evident in the name of the narrator, John Neverbend, who tells his story of how, as president of the island, he tried to enforce the law once the first member of its young population reached the required age. He is a zealot, sensitive and caring but a zealot nevertheless, always reminding himself that other great benefactors of humanity, Galileo and Columbus being his prime examples, had also suffered for their beliefs, and convinced that whatever personal discomforts he has to endure are trivial in comparison with the benefits that adoption of his scheme will eventually bring to humanity as a whole. In some ways, therefore, the novel is in a line of satirical writing stretching back to Swift's *Modest Proposal for Preventing the Children of Poor People from Being a Burthen to Their Parents or Country*; yet, whereas no one but a psychopath could actually believe that encouraging Irish mothers to sell their babies so that they could be eaten by their richer compatriots was a good idea, euthanasia, at least in the form of what we now refer to as assisted suicide, has a lot to be said for it.

Trollope makes this clear as Neverbend struggles with the fact that the first person on the island to reach the qualifying age for participation in the scheme is a close friend, that this friend happens to be in decent health, and that his daughter, with whom his own son is in love, vehemently objects to losing her father. These all too human complications eventually defeat Neverbend's efforts to have the law implemented but the description of the folly of having a cut-off point for everyone, as well as of the psychological distress that comes from individuals knowing precisely when their own cut-off point is going to be, does not stop Trollope from indicating that, in the right circumstances, providing people with a comfortable exit from this world is a humane and rational procedure. Moreover, if he makes fun of Neverbend's doctrinaire intransigence, he also writes satirically about the hide-bound notions of the upper-class figures who are sent from Britain to remove him from the island's presidency and take the island back under imperial control, people for whom the old ways are always and inevitably the best.

By the time *The Fixed Period* was published, Dickens had been dead more than ten years. With his linguistic exuberance and interest in the grotesque, he was a very different kind of writer from Trollope and worked from different models. One of these was Ben Jonson, whom he greatly admired, much more so than George Eliot, yet it was she who, in *Middlemarch*, created the nearest, well-known nineteenth-century equivalent of Volpone. Peter Featherstone is a rich farmer, who does not have the vitality of his literary predecessor, and he is not merely pretending to be on his last legs; but he has gathered round a similar group of individuals who are anxious for him to die so that they will know how his considerable wealth is going to be distributed. These are relatives old Peter delights in keeping in suspense as they visit him regularly so that he can be reminded not to leave his money 'out of the family'. Looking after him is a young woman called Mary Garth, who is like old Martin Chuzzlewit's Mary Graham in having no, or very few, expectations. She is being courted by Peter's nephew, Fred Vincy. Having been sent to Oxford by his aspiring parents, he is faced with the prospect of a career in the Church, when he would much rather be the gentleman farmer that inheriting Peter's land would allow him to become. In the event, he and all Peter's other relatives are disappointed when it turns out that he has left part of his estate to charity, and his farm to a frog-faced young man whom no one in Middlemarch has ever seen before but who is later identified as his illegitimate son. Peter can be imagined as having anticipated with glee the shock and surprise that his own version of family loyalty occasions, even though he cannot be present in person to enjoy it.

George Eliot deals with many different levels of small-town society in *Middlemarch*. At its apex, as all its readers remember, is Dorothea Brooke who is attracted to a rich clergyman and scholar, much older than herself, because she naïvely imagines he has a great mind and that, as his wife, she will be able to help him complete the important work on which he is engaged. No one is better than Eliot at showing how egotism can operate in even an individual as decent and scrupulous as Dorothea, who is drawn to an idealised notion of participating in some major intellectual endeavour, like one of Milton's daughters reading to her blind father. Once actually married to Casaubon, however, she has a growing sense of having made a fatal mistake. One unfortunate effect of her slow change of heart is to feed her husband's his own self-doubt about the value of this work. Tormented by the role Dorothea has inadvertently played in making him realise that he may have wasted his life, but also, and even more crucially, by his awareness of how much less at ease she is with him than with Will Ladislaw, his young impecunious relative, he makes a will in which he leaves most of his wealth to his widow, but only on condition that she does not marry Ladislaw.

This effort of Casaubon's to extend his power into the future fails when, after his death, Dorothea and Will decide they have no need of his money anyway. It is hard to control events *in absentia*, as Dr Sloper is made to realise in *Washington Square*, or even in the last stages of life. My previous account would appear to suggest that Peter Featherstone had succeeded in doing so but in fact he has written two wills and, just before dying, tries to persuade Mary Garth to help him destroy one of them because he has become too feeble to act on his own. 'I've made everything ready to change my mind', he says 'and do as I like at the last.' Mary is aware that the will Peter now wants to preserve contains benefits for Fred Vincy, whom she loves, but she resists her employer's entreaties to help him, and his offer of money, anxious as she is not to be 'open to suspicion', so that the old and dying man discovers that he cannot do as he likes after all. As I have implied, relatives who are asked to increase the morphine dose of a dying parent whose heirs they are might well feel they are in a position similar to hers.

Wills are not always the simple instruments of power that they might seem. Max Brod was the devoted friend of Kafka but, as Ian Hamilton has pointed out, his devotion did not stop him ignoring the explicit instructions in Kafka's will that all his unpublished manuscripts should be destroyed. He was not the first to leave behind a request of this kind. Not all writers are like Stendhal and willing to allow everything they have written take its chance in the future. Many are anxious to retain that control after death which, during their lifetimes, has allowed them only to offer to the public what they finally feel, after many corrections, are their best efforts. In this, they are a little like those of us who were told by our mothers to change our underwear regularly in case we were ever run over, even though, if we were lying wounded and unconscious on a hospital operating table, it could hardly have mattered to us whether the doctors concerned were critical of our personal hygiene. In a similar way, the judgement that an unfinished novel or poem falls below its author's usual standard can hardly be upsetting to a writer who is dead. Yet perhaps it is wrong to make light of these worries. When he knew he was dying, Robert Burns is reported to have regretted that:

> he had written ... many indifferent poetical pieces, which he feared would now, with all their imperfections on their head, be thrust upon the world. On this account he deeply regretted having deferred to put his papers into a state of arrangement, as he was now quite incapable of the exertion.[3]

Those bonfires that some writers are known to have lit before their death were no doubt usually designed to frustrate biographers, but they may sometimes also have been meant to ensure that a writer should look his or her best when appearing before the bar of future public opinion.

There have been several instances in which the example of Max Brod in relation to Kafka has been followed and the explicit wishes of the deceased ignored. In the vast majority of cases there are, of course, no problems, but sometimes the law itself is not always on the side of those who might want to have their own way and make, for example, special provision for those they leave behind. Throughout almost the whole of British legal history there have been what are sometimes called 'entails' on large estates. These often stipulated that the property could not be broken up but must be passed on to the nearest surviving male relative so that anyone who held it at any particular time was really doing so in a kind of trust. The insistence on gender was to avoid the danger of the estate falling under the control of a different family but it is no surprise that its unfairness caught the eye of another of the nineteenth

---

3. From Ian Hamilton, *Keepers of the Flame*.

century's great female novelists. At the beginning of Jane Austen's *Sense and Sensibility*, the Dashwood estate has been transferred to John Dashwood, the nearest male relative, to the exclusion of the deceased owner's widow and daughters. As the son of that owner by a previous marriage, he initially feels a moral obligation to make some kind of supplementary financial provision for his stepmother and half-sisters, who are the victims of a legal system weighted against women. From a starting point of large sums of money, the reader is invited by Austen to look on in ironic amusement as he and his mercenary wife give themselves apparently respectable reasons for eventually narrowing down that provision to a 'few neighbourly acts'. More familiar to readers will be the entail which, in *Pride and Prejudice*, means that if Mr Bennet dies his estate will not go to his widow and daughters but to the odious Mr Collins whose offer to make amends for the unfairness, by marrying into the family, is less of a relief than a threat to the novel's heroine. This situation has a potential starting-point which her father has no more power to do anything about than the deceased Mr Dashwood had to protect the female members of his immediate family.

Looking back on these legal arrangements, they often seem iniquitous or at least to be productive of iniquitous results but it is possible that they could sometimes have had beneficial effects. It was partly the workings of male primogeniture that plucked Jane Austen's brother Edward from his relatively modest surroundings in order to become the head of several large estates, with the only price he had to pay being a change of name (from Austen to Knight). This meant that she could periodically observe and to some extent enjoy the benefits of an aristocratic lifestyle in contrast to her more straightened circumstances at home. Meanwhile, during roughly the same period, Percy Bysshe Shelley wrote a pamphlet in defence of atheism that resulted in his being sent down from Oxford, after which he married against his family's wishes. His father would no doubt have liked to disinherit him but there was an entail on the family estate that prevented him from doing so. The result was that Shelley could maintain a reasonably extravagant lifestyle by borrowing money against his future financial expectations and look forward to being rich when his father died. That he then drowned when he was 30, while his father survived into his nineties, is an example of those ironies of which Hardy was so fond, yet these are exceptional cases and in ordinary life matters no doubt proceeded, and still do proceed, more smoothly, especially as the majority of people have usually had precious little to leave or, in our day, have had what they once did possess whittled down by the cost of care.

For those who do still have money, property or possessions to leave behind, the will is not only a potential means of power but can also operate as a public revelation of character. Difficult as it is to estimate how far Shakespeare, in his own endlessly discussed will, was simply doing what was expected of him as a Jacobean gentleman, it does appear to reveal something of his attitude to his wife and daughters, while its numerous individual bequests at least tell us who, at the end of his life, he considered his best friends, either in the local Stratford community or amongst the theatrical fraternity. To a number of former actor colleagues, such as Heminge and Condell, for example, the two men who would be responsible for publishing the collection of his plays known as the First Folio in 1623, as well as to various friends nearer home, Shakespeare left the traditional two marks so that they could all buy what are known as mourning rings. That this was so much a convention of the time means that it is impossible to know how far Shakespeare was the kind of person so anxious to be remembered that he was providing the money for a memento that would recall him to mind every time his friends looked down at their fingers – although, in that case, he could never have been entirely certain that the rings would always be worn. Catherine Richardson, in an essay on commemoration in early modern England entitled '"Make you a cloak of it and weare it for my sake"', has unearthed the will of a sheriff of Canterbury who in 1597 left this kind of gift to his executors with the accompanying instruction that they were to meet formally once a year and thus provide an event, she says, 'at which the wearing of those rings could become part of a ritual, public display of memory and association'. Since one example of the rings she is talking about, which is now in the V&A, has a grinning skull as its centrepiece, a reminder of not only the benefactor's death but the inevitability of its wearer's own, one can see why they might only have been put on for special occasions.[4] As Shakespeare left no instructions in his will about when his friends should wear their rings, it does not much help to lift the veil on the vexed question of 'what he was really like', although he did also leave ten pounds for the poor. Alas, the jury is still out on whether this sum, for a man of his means, entitles us to consider him as either mean or generous.

Wills of a more recent vintage than Shakespeare's are likely to be easier to interpret so that the opportunity they offer of a final address to the world can also turn out to reveal more than those who make them might

---

4. The V&A experts confidently claim that it is to this kind of ring Falstaff is referring when he begs Doll Tearsheet not to talk to him like a death's head and remind him of his end (see Chapter 1 above).

have wanted the world to know while they were still alive. Casaubon is a fictional figure but his feelings must have been like those of many men in Victorian England who had married much younger wives and cast a jealous eye on what their widows might get up to once they were gone. It was not as if they were living in a country where a bereaved spouse would be expected to throw herself on the funeral pyre. His stipulation that Dorothea can only inherit his wealth if she refrains from marrying Will Ladislaw shocks the upper-class circle in Middlemarch to which he belongs; but that may be chiefly because it implies there might have been something improper about the relationship between Dorothea and Will whilst he was still alive (a conclusion which the ending of the novel suggests that, according to Casaubon's own lights, there indeed was). He would have been ashamed to reveal his jealousy while he was living but can perhaps be thought of as calculating that being dead would save him from the embarrassment. On the whole, what many wills show is an anxiety to make a favourable impression, not only in the immediate prelude to death but also after it has taken place. They suggest a reliance on scenarios the dead person is not in a position to know will ever occur. Casaubon may be a counter-example to this common urge by showing himself prepared to reveal feelings he would have been ashamed to express to others while he was still living, but can freely indulge once he is safely out of the way. When ageing individuals sit down to make their wills, one of their preoccupations may sometimes be the need to be thought well of after their deaths, but there will always be some who do not care about that, or who are conscious of how limited any individual's control over a post-mortem reputation is likely to be.

Recruiting Office, 1914
Photograph from the *Daily Mirror*

8

Nostalgia

Nostalgia and old people tend to go together, as a quick look through any issue of such a successful publication as *The Oldie* will attest; but the two have not always and inevitably been associated. The term was first coined in the late seventeenth century by a Swiss medical student from two Greek words, *nostos* meaning homecoming and *algos* pain or ache. It was principally used to describe the homesickness that afflicted the student's fellow countrymen when they went abroad to seek work in foreign armies as mercenaries. The important point is that for him it was quite clearly a disease. One of his successors even tried to a provide a biological basis for nostalgia by suggesting it was caused by the pressure on the brain when those who had been brought up in the Alps had to live and work in (for example) the *Low* Countries.

Over the years, this yearning for home came to mean also any kind of longing to return to, and enjoy, a former state, one version of which Freud was to particularise as regression. Its many and varied manifestations have attracted the interest of both psychologists and social scientists, and there is now a team in Southampton who are conducting psychological experiments in order to study its effects.[1] For those like Owen Hatherley who are concerned with politics, nostalgia has also been important since it can have an important influence on voting patterns, not least perhaps in the recent debate in Great Britain over membership of the European Union. He points out that, in the 1997 British General Election,

---

1. My information about the Southampton group comes mainly from Clay Routledge in his *Nostalgia: A Psychological Resource* (2016). Other information on the topic can be found in Svetlana Boym's *The Future of Nostalgia* (2001).

the manifesto of the Monster Raving Loony Party, an organisation not usually noted for its acuity, promised to set up a 'Ministry of Nostalgia'. This was because, they said, 'we all need help to dream of a wonderful bygone age when everyone was paid in golden sovereigns, no one was ill or died, the weather was perfect, and you could get 200 pints of beer for a quid'.

Nostalgic feelings have always been important and there is a good example of what they might mean for individuals of any age in an early poem by D.H. Lawrence entitled 'Piano'. This describes how the narrator is listening to a woman singing, 'in the dusk', and the way her voice takes him back to a time when he was a small child and sitting under the family piano, touching the feet of his mother who was also singing. The effect of 'the insidious mastery of song' is to make him yearn for 'the old Sunday evenings at home, with winter outside / And hymns in the cosy parlour, the tinkling piano our guide'. When, therefore, the woman to whom he is listening changes the mood and begins to sing more loudly, it is too late because 'the glamour of childish days' is upon him, his 'manhood' is 'cast down' with the result that, in spite of himself, he can only 'weep like a child for the past'.

The trigger for this outburst of nostalgia is auditory and an illustration of the involuntary memory that so preoccupied Proust. In his case, the most well-known example is gustatory – the taste of a cake known in France as a *madeleine* – but his narrator is also carried back down what Lawrence calls the 'vista of years' by sounds, particular sights or even the physical sensation of tripping on a pavement as he is entering that afternoon musical party given by the Guermantes. For him, that the body is a repository of past experiences that can be made available by their accidental replication in the present constitutes a triumph over the inexorable onward movement of chronological time and is a recovery of that lost past to which the title of Proust's novel refers.

'Piano' had an interesting history because it was chosen by I.A. Richards as one of thirteen examples of short poems in his *Practical Criticism*, a book that was to have a significant impact on how English literature would be taught in British universities for the 40 or so years after its publication. What Richards did was gather together a mixture of Cambridge undergraduates and doctoral students, together with the odd colleague, and ask them to write down their considered responses to these poems, the crucial factor being that he did not reveal who their authors were. 'Piano' was number eight on his list but it came even lower down in the popularity stakes. This was partly because several respondents misread it or introduced inappropriate criteria, criticising its author for having a poor taste in music, for example, or characterising the situation it described as 'sordid' (and then praising Lawrence for having found such appropriately 'unpoetical' words to describe it). But the main reason seemed to be the feeling that any poem involving childhood reminiscence must necessarily be sentimental: 'Silly, maudlin, sentimental twaddle' was one verdict, 'wallowing in a bath of soapy sentiment' another. Given that the majority of Richards' guinea pigs were young, it is perhaps not surprising that they were quick to seize on and denounce any hint of nostalgia. In his own commentary, Richards defends the poem by pointing out that Lawrence is not too keen on it either (the mastery of song is 'insidious' and it is in spite of himself that he is transported back into the past), although whether this makes any difference to the poem's quality is questionable. What Richards appears to assume, just like his young guinea pigs, is that nostalgia is on the whole a bad thing and he gives Lawrence brownie points for struggling against it. That he would have been justified in doing so, in Lawrence's own eyes at least, is suggested by lines from an earlier version of 'Piano' that became available in the three-volume 2013 edition of his poems and which read: 'And the black piano is clamouring as my mother's never could clamour; / And I hate the past, oh I hate the past's dead glamour'.

One reason why the feelings described in 'Piano' tend to be more characteristic of the old than of those of Lawrence's years when he wrote the poem is that, with age, the memory of recent events tends to weaken while that of earlier times becomes sharper. Recently, the psychologists in Southampton I mentioned have tended towards thinking that *indulging* in nostalgia (my choice of verb indicates the usual negative charge of the noun) may not be such a bad thing after all, especially for those who are unlike the Swiss mercenaries in not having to get up every morning in order to assert what in 'Piano' is referred to as 'manhood'. This is in part because one curious aspect of nostalgia it is that, although it can generate sadness, enough to make someone like Lawrence weep, it is usually also pleasurable. When the main female character returns to what used to be the nursery of her family home in *The Cherry Orchard*, Chekhov describes her as speaking 'joyfully, through her tears'. As his plays so often demonstrate, nostalgia is 'a bittersweet emotion', to borrow the words of one of those scientists involved in studying it. For this expert, it is 'more sweet than bitter' because the feelings of loss and sadness it evokes are 'outweighed by positive emotions'. There may be regret at the disappearance of former times but there is also comfort in being able to revisit and, in some sense, re-inhabit them. If Lawrence weeps like a child for the past, he is also experiencing some sad enjoyment in recalling a time when he was close to his mother.

It is with the Romantics, in particular, that childhood becomes one of those home territories to which one can lovingly look back. Wordsworth again offers a prime example here. Christianity appears to have played no deeply integral part in the early years of Wordsworth's life and he seems to have grown up largely unaffected by Christian doctrine, happy to elaborate his own idiosyncratic theology. Where this can be seen most clearly is in what is usually known as his 'Immortality Ode'. In conventional Christianity, life is a journey or pilgrimage towards a future state that will be everlasting. Wordsworth puts this process into reverse and claims in his poem that children arrive in this world *from* some kind of previous paradisal region, 'trailing clouds of glory'. According to him, we all have memories of this previous existence that presumably help to explain why, when we are young, everything appears 'Apparelled in celestial light'. Gradually, however, as we grow older, the 'visionary gleam' fades and we plod on into 'the light of common day'. With views like this, it is hardly surprising that Wordsworth should have had strong nostalgic feelings about the time when he was a child in the Lake District or that the record suggests he was a gloomy old man.

The idea that it is only in the late eighteenth and early nineteenth centuries when childhood came to be valued is probably as open to as many counter-examples as the belief that, in early modern England, parents did not become attached to their children because the rate of infant mortality was so high. In his 'Ode on a Distant Prospect of Eton College', Thomas Gray, who died in 1771, looks nostalgically back to his own boyhood, although his emphasis falls not so much on its pleasures than on the blissful ignorance the child enjoys of what life will have in store: 'regardless of their doom, / The little victims play!' One way in which nostalgia of this kind can become a collective phenomenon is illustrated in a much better known poem by Gray. 'Oft did the harvest to their sickle yield, / Their furrow oft the stubborn glebe has broke', he writes in his famous 'Elegy Written in a Country Churchyard', 'How jocund did they drive their team afield! / How bow'd the woods beneath their sturdy stroke!' No amount of sophistication about pastoral conventions will stop some readers feeling that Gray's 'rude forefathers' cannot always have been jocund, or that there must occasionally have been a tree that was to them what the recalcitrant old stump is to Wordsworth's Simon Lee. It was in implicit criticism of this kind of idealisation of country life that Wordsworth called his 'Michael' a pastoral. Nostalgic though he might have been about his own childhood, he was too close an observer of rural life not to be aware of the differences between loving the countryside and trying to extract a living from it, even if he explicitly argues in 'Michael' that the two can be combined.

People can become nostalgic about certain modes of economic activity, especially if they themselves were associated with them when they were young, but also certain periods of time. It is striking, for example, how often writers of the 1920s and 1930s looked back to the Edwardian era as a golden age. This was largely because the period was being viewed through the prism of the First World War when they, or others like them, were then in the same situation as Gray's Etonians and 'regardless of the coming doom'. There is a later and modified version of this perspective in Philip Larkin's 1960 poem 'MCMXIV'. This begins with a description of an old photograph showing a straggly line of men with 'moustached archaic faces' outside a recruiting office in 1914, looking as if they are going to a football or cricket match, or are on 'An August Bank Holiday lark'. It then widens out to evoke nostalgically, although perhaps also ironically, the England of that time, with (among other features) its old coinage, children named after members of the royal family and a countryside still dominated by large houses with their train of domestic servants. 'Never such innocence, / Never before or since,' Larkin comments and ends his short poem with 'Never such innocence again.' Yet the only reason why the lost world he describes was innocent is that it did not have the benefit of the hindsight he enjoys: in all other respects it was probably an age no more innocent than any other. The thought his poem provokes is that one of the explanations for the enjoyment some individuals can find in nostalgia is that it involves looking back to a time when they still had hopes, which they did not then know would later be disappointed.

Nostalgia can be experienced at almost any age but the older one gets, the more opportunities there are for it to surface and one of the best illustrations of this comes in Shakespeare's *King Henry IV: Part 2*. Falstaff is on a recruiting mission in Gloucestershire and about to call on an old acquaintance called Robert Shallow, who is a Justice of the Peace and responsible, along with a relative called Silence, also a JP, for drawing up a list of men from which the recruits can be chosen. The crucial scene begins with Shallow asking his colleague about his family and, when he is told that Silence's son is at Oxford ('to my cost'), he notes that it must be about time for the young man to move on to the Inns of Court in London in order to study law, as he himself had done 50 or so years before: 'I was once of Clement's Inn, where I think they will talk of mad Shallow yet.' This leads him to reminisce about his friends from student days, all the pranks he got up to, the prostitutes he knew and the fights he had: 'Jesu, Jesu, the mad days that I have spent!' It is the apparently carefree nature of his student life that he enjoys remembering, now that he is a solid, prosperous citizen with responsibilities.

When Falstaff then enters, there is a comic interlude in which the ludicrously inadequate group of potential recruits Shallow and Silence have provided for him are inspected (later he will choose only those not prepared to offer bribes to keep themselves off the list); but he then joins Shallow in recalling their student days together. At the beginning of the scene Shallow had distracted himself from the uncomfortable thought of how many of those he once knew are now dead by immediately juxtaposing his enquiries after them with questions to Silence about the price of beef and lamb at the local market. Now, however, he asks Falstaff if Jane Nightwork, a prostitute who could 'not abide' him, is still alive and is told that she is holding her own but 'old, old, Master Shallow'. Yet the times 'this knight and I have seen', he then says to Silence, allowing Falstaff (who is the knight in question) to contribute what is the most frequently quoted line from this scene, 'We have heard the chimes at midnight, Master Shallow.'

In performance, this scene with Shallow and Silence is almost always successful but its humour and pathos are hard to illustrate in print because they depend so much on the exchange of simple words: Jane Nightwork must be old, Shallow reflects, 'she cannot choose but be old; … and had Robin Nightwork by old Nightwork before I came to Clement's Inn.' As someone always more interested in the present than the past, Falstaff is a reluctant participant in Shallow's reminiscing and, in his final summing up, what he suggests is that his old acquaintance has been giving a far more impressive picture of himself as a young man than the reality justifies. Shallow was actually, he says, a wholly insignificant figure in those court circles where we have now learnt that Falstaff himself had been a page to the Duke of Norfolk; and also physically puny and thin (although who wouldn't be in comparison with this particular speaker?). 'And now has he land and beef', Falstaff complains like someone whose life has come to very little and then suddenly discovers that a boy he had hardly noticed at school is a company director. Reflecting on Shallow's idea of himself as a madcap, he exclaims, 'Lord, Lord, how subject we old men are to this vice of lying!' Lying is a topic on which Falstaff could be said to be an authority but it is of course true that, if the nostalgic version of the past which old men and women entertain should not be called mendacious, it is at least nearly always severely edited. How otherwise to explain how *some* of those who are looking back to periods spent in an impoverished family, boarding school or the armed forces, where material conditions were harsh, persist in regarding them as the happiest times of their lives?

This problem of truth raised by Falstaff affects not only nostalgia but all retrospection, and especially, therefore, all autobiography. Rousseau insisted at the beginning of his *Confessions* that his work was unique in its 'unparalleled truthfulness' and Gibbon began his autobiography with, 'Truth, naked, unblushing truth, the first virtue of more serious history, must be the sole recommendation of this personal narrative.' In striking a similar note, Stendhal wisely claimed, in his own autobiography, that what he had to say was the truth, *as far as he could know it*. Aware of how deceptive memory can be, subsequent autobiographers have followed this lead, in part to distinguish their own writings from pseudo-autobiographies like those of Defoe;[2] but Clive James, a much more recent contributor to the genre, took a different tack. In the preface to the first volume of his autobiography, significantly entitled *Unreliable Memoirs*, he said that what followed was 'a disguised novel' and that 'really the whole affair is a figment got up to sound like the truth'. That was because, he went on, he had been careful to spare other people's feelings and, if he had been even more careful *not* to spare his own (which was Rousseau's claim about his *Confessions*), it was only 'up … to a point'. This is important in at least hinting at categories to which the criterion of truth or truthfulness could usefully apply; but it surely gives too many hostages to fortune. Did James really want his readers to regard as a figment of his imagination his claim that his father, a former prisoner of the Japanese, died when the plane in which he was being repatriated, crashed just after the Second World War was over; or that he was then brought up by his widowed mother in a Sydney suburb where there was very little money around?

This problem of truth in autobiography can be seen to intersect with those of old age when in 2010 Clive James was diagnosed with leukaemia. Five years later, he published a collection of poems entitled *Sentenced to Life* that he fully expected to be his last. One of these is called 'Japanese Maple' and was very well received. It begins with a recognition by James that his death is now near but he says that he hopes to survive at least until the autumn when the tree's leaves will 'turn to flame'. In an

---

2. *Moll Flanders*.

interview with Mary Beard, which appeared on television in 2019, James commented wryly on the fact that news of his death had turned out to be exaggerated and, asked about the Japanese maple, was able to report with a smile that it was the tree that had died while he was still hanging on. 'Japanese Maple' is clearly autobiographical but no one has suggested that the details in it are invented even if James' life lasted longer than he expected it would. He went on writing poems until his death at the end of 2019 and in many of them details of his family background abound that are authentic in the sense of verifiable. A collection he published in 2017, which, no doubt inadvertently, has the same title as his friend Enright's final book, includes a poem called 'The Smocking Block' that describes the intricacy of the needlework his mother undertook to supplement the family income and compares it with the care involved in writing poems. Although I have not myself verified this detail, it is hard to believe it could be one merely got up to 'sound like the truth'.

What is obviously necessary is a categorisation of the details about which autobiographers are likely not to be telling the absolute truth either because the memory is fallible or, as T.S. Eliot once put it (in an essay on *Othello*), and despite all Rousseau's protestations to the contrary, 'nothing dies harder than the desire to think well of oneself'. There is also the pressure on any author to adapt his material to a particular literary form. In that striking episode involving the decayed gibbet to which I refer at the beginning of this book, there are details that no Wordsworth scholar has yet been able to bring into strict alignment with the available historical and biographical evidence. Lawrence's memory of sitting under the piano as a small child while his mother played and sang may be authentic but it is not an incident that could have taken place in his own home since, as far as we can know, his family did not acquire a piano until he was fourteen. Of course, it is possible that having to write poetry rather than prose puts an unusual pressure on the facts as any particular poet chooses to recall them. Peering into the past is in any event always a tricky affair and no more so than when the people and episodes involved are evoked nostalgically since nostalgia is a version of former times with most of the unpleasant aspects of experience left out or transformed.

That a nostalgic version of the past tends to be partial and therefore false is one of the reasons why nostalgia has a bad reputation among literary commentators and I.A. Richards can praise Lawrence for struggling against it. The hero of *Lucky Jim*, a novel by Kingsley Amis, which had a great success in the 1960s, is a young medievalist who finds himself obliged to give a public lecture. For various reasons, including the ingestion of too much whisky, he begins to feel ill as he is speaking but, before collapsing on the platform he manages to blurt out, 'What, finally, is the practical application of all this? Listen and I'll tell you. The point about Merrie England is that it was about the most un-Merrie period in our history.' He is protesting against a sanitised view of the pre-industrial past, crowded with Morris dancers, handicrafts and jocund ploughmen that he feels his professor espouses and suggesting that the 'good old days' were rarely as good as all that. This is almost always true whether in the course of history generally or in that of an individual life. There may well have been a time when it was far easier to visit a family doctor but, with the progress in medical science, the one you do eventually manage to see is in a position to do far more for a patient than his predecessors. Beer was certainly much cheaper in the past but not in comparison to average incomes and, though it would be a relief to be spared the horrors of a modern airport or congestion on the roads, getting from A to B is on average now far quicker than it used to be. Looking back responsibly is a delicate and often rigorous matter of weighing pros and cons with which nostalgia has nothing to do. Shallow is an old man who lies because of a fundamental regret about no longer being young and also because of the shadow of death that he feels is all around him.

Following on from her *Aging and Its Discontents: Freud and Other Fictions*, the psychoanalytic critic Kathleen Woodward wrote an essay in which she aimed to distinguish between what she called the life review (which I refer to in my next chapter as 'taking stock') and reminiscence. She explained that her major interest was in 'the emotional state that accompanies reminiscence and the function of that emotional state'. Claiming that when we reminisce 'we are less concerned with finding the truth than we are in creating a certain atmosphere', one that is 'generative and restorative', she cited the psychoanalyst Helene Deutsch who had suggested that 'whether the facts associated with a memory are accurate is not the point: what is important is the *feeling* of the memory, the memory of the *feeling*'. Deutsch had noted, Woodward explains, that there was 'an 'emotional bias' in what she remembered in which, as she herself put it, 'the negative elements are often omitted' with the result that the memories became 'more supportive, more protective'.

That the problem of truth can be brushed aside so easily by a psychoanalyst seems at first at little surprising when the origins of her own science or art can be found in Freud's far from immediate recognition that the stories his patients told him about being sexually abused by their fathers were, in fact, not true, but rather fantasies that would then help him to develop the founding concept of the Oedipus complex. Whether or not the memories any analyst manages to elicit in a session are make-believe strikes me also as more of a problem than is generally acknowledged, and yet, that thorny issue aside, there seems nothing especially wrong about a group of old men and women sitting round a table reflecting nostalgically on their past lives, perhaps with the aid of photographs, those potent sources of pleasant memories. It may be, therefore, that the reporter on the experiments in Southampton is right to refer to nostalgia as a valuable psychological resource, an 'existential utility' that can 'mitigate the effects of death-related cognition', and to suggest that it performs an important function in boosting positive self-regard and enhancing feelings of self-worth. Yet what if the self-worth concerned has no more justification than that of Shallow, in Falstaff's judgement on him? A doctor in the American Civil War, whom Clay Routledge quotes, kept up the tradition of those who first talked of nostalgia as an illness by noting that the young men who were suffering from it could be bullied out of the condition by their fellow soldiers and that 'an active campaign, with attendant marches and more particularly its battles, is the best curative' for what was 'a shameful disease that revealed a lack of manliness and unprogressive attitudes'. This is an approach to nostalgia that no one is likely to recommend today and besides, as the world moves forward, there are surely aspects of living the disappearance of which the old have a perfect right to lament because they represent genuine loss: practices and attitudes that have only an incidental relation to their own personal lives and can therefore provide an entirely legitimate focus for regret. Yet the difficulty remains of knowing whether, in appearing to mourn their passing (of the old way of teaching English literature, for example), what is in fact exciting nostalgic longing is one's own lost youth. One of the shrewdest features of Swift's account of the Struldbruggs is his suggestion that as they age they cease to understand the language of even their own country. Most people who revisit the factory, office or institution where they once worked are likely to have an inkling of what he meant and recognise that one of the discomforts of old age is falling out of tune with the idiom of the generations below. 'The times they are a-changin'', sang Bob Dylan, in what was once a popular anthem of youth, and he advised the old to get out of the way 'if you can't lend your hand'. Whether any particular change is for good or bad, and represents a real improvement, cannot

Nostalgia 99

be easily answered but what seems certain is that nostalgia is not much help for those old people who think it worthwhile to try to make that determination, however much it may assist in warding off what, in the unappealing language of the social scientists, is referred to as 'death-related cognition'.

The Last Judgement
Painting by Albrecht Dürer from *The Small Passion*, c. 1510.
Metropolitan Museum of Art, New York

9

Taking Stock

Nostalgia is only one particular way we have of recalling the past. There are also moments in people's lives, often towards the end of them, when they are prompted to review what has gone before and take stock. One mood in which this task is undertaken is encapsulated in a song made popular by Frank Sinatra. This is called 'My Way' and begins with, 'And now, the end is near / And so I face the final curtain'. It may be later words in this song which are being recalled by the Australian painter Jeffrey Smart when he was interviewed for her book by Irma Kurtz and invited to look back on his life. 'Oh yes, I have regrets', Smart said:

> Why didn't I go off with that person? Why didn't I go to bed with another? Or why didn't I buy shares in that company? Or why was I so suspicious of that estate agent? Why did I think he was a crook when it turns out he was right and I was wrong? There's a lot of that in life.

In former times, the responsibility for taking stock of life was in part taken out of the hands of individuals by anticipation of what was known as the Last Judgement. With Purgatory still in play, this was a slightly more comfortable prospect than when its consequences became more binary and stark. With the decline of religion, and belief in the afterlife, the responsibility for some kind of final summing-up passed to autobiography, along with a good deal of the seriousness that operation implied. In the case of Smart, however, the seriousness seems to have drained away and left a series of past life choices chiefly remarkable for their triviality.

The autobiography of Stendhal is one of the best books he ever wrote (and certainly the best that remained unpublished at his death). It begins by his asking just what kind of person he has been. By the time everything is all over in two or three years, he says, describing his life will have taught him whether his character was fundamentally gay or sad, what his intellectual capabilities were, whether he was courageous or cowardly and could think of himself as having been happy or miserable. But the chief question that preoccupies him is whether he could be said to have had any real talent. 'If there is another world,' he claims (in spite of his later prediction about the fame he would enjoy in 1880), 'I shan't fail to go and see Montesquieu. If he says, "My poor friend, you haven't any talent whatsoever", I'll be annoyed but not at all surprised.' Wordsworth is a great writer but one can make an important qualification about his genius by imagining the expression on his face if he received the same news.

Two major questions that lie behind very many others that autobiographers are inclined to ask are: 'Has my life been meaningful?' and 'Has it been a success?' Dealing with the second of these is hard without making comparisons with other people, looking at the achievements of what Shakespeare calls in Sonnet 29 'this man's art, and that man's scope'. In certain areas comparison is futile but, whereas there is not much point in regretting that we are not (as Shakespeare puts it in the line above the one I quote) 'featured' like someone else, it would be more reasonable to reproach ourselves if, towards the end of our lives, we are not 'with friends possessed'. Did we make the most of the advantages we enjoyed when we compare ourselves with others who had very similar starting-points, when we were, for example, schoolchildren or students together? It is a question of how we value ourselves and what we have achieved in life. On this issue of value, Hobbes is characteristically hard-nosed in *Leviathan*, insisting that, 'For let a man (as most men do,) rate themselves at the highest Value they can; yet their true Value is no more than it is esteemed by others.' On the other hand, when the chief value concerned is a matter of writing, or art in general, as it was for Stendhal, for example, then it becomes reasonable to ask who these others are who are in charge of the estimation to which Hobbes refers. A majority view may not in fact turn out to be the lasting one, and an artist's contemporaries may not always be the best judges of his or her work, which is where that 'posterity' I have already discussed comes in.

Someone who might well have asked himself how his own work would eventually be evaluated, in comparison with that of his contemporaries, is Paul Cézanne. Rejected by the Paris art establishment, he retreated to his native Provence and doggedly pursued his own line. If his father had not been wealthy, it is doubtful whether he could have carried on being a painter. By the time he died, he had a few devoted admirers but was regarded as bafflingly eccentric by a majority in the art world. The challenge he must have represented for his contemporaries was described by D.W. Harding in his 1941 work, *The Impulse to Dominate*, as distinguishing between 'a valuable persistence in individual development and the stubbornness of worthless self-conceit'. That question is always unfortunately with us and it is some version of it that seems to have been in Stendhal's mind as he began his autobiography, especially as, unlike Cézanne, he never married and could not therefore look to a family as proof that his life had not been without meaning. Unlike his later compatriot, Stendhal did have a conventional profession but, after a period during the Napoleonic Empire when it seemed as if he might achieve great things, his career had stalled and, whereas his former close friend, Félix Faure, with whom he had been at school, was now a senator and member of the French State Council, he himself was stuck by the 1830s in that dead-end job of French consul in Civitavecchia. By this stage, therefore, all his eggs were in the literary basket, which is why the question of his putative talent must have been so important to him.

Comparison with others can be important when individuals are taking stock of their lives, and so too can the counterfactual. 'Regrets, I've had a few', sings Sinatra in the line to which Jeffrey Smart seems to allude. What would have happened had I not gone to that school, missed out on military service, been born in another country, not married that girl, taken that offer of a job …? The speculations are endless and most of them also quite pointless. This is in part because individuals who ask 'if only' have to do so from the position they presently occupy, whereas, if the life-changing event they imagine had in fact taken place, it would have been likely to produce other alterations in themselves and their situations that are incalculable. Imagine you are in a supermarket, a philosopher friend once suggested,[1] and you emerge from the aisles alongside another shopper. The two of you decide to join different queues but yours, which initially looked like being shorter, is delayed by an old lady's trouble in finding her purse or a change of cashier. The result is that, by the time you come to pay, the other shopper has left the building. You can then say with certainty that, if I had only joined the other queue, I would

---

1. Frank Cioffi.

have been quicker. Yet there are rather more important life choices, involving, for example, schools, husbands, or jobs, that cannot be tested in such limited, controlled circumstances.

When 'what if' questions are listed under the heading of regrets, it is because they are being asked by people who look back with a measure of dissatisfaction but there are those who are perfectly happy to rest easy when they think about their past lives. Edward Gibbon was one of these and so much so that there is an issue about whether the tone in his autobiography should be described as contented or smug. Cummings is someone who opted firmly for the latter description (he thought that Gibbon's tone was like that of Jane Austen's Mr Collins) but then the two men were in very different situations as regards money, health and success. Gibbon had occasional anxieties about his income but on the whole was very well provided for; as he says himself, after a difficult childhood he almost never had to see a doctor. As for success, his history of the decline and fall of the Roman Empire had made him famous all over Europe. Yet here is also the question of temperament. 'My temper', he says at one point, 'is not very susceptible of enthusiasm' and a few pages later he also acquits it of envy. When he was first sent to Lausanne by his father, he fell in love with a beautiful and gifted girl (who was later to become the wife of the celebrated Swiss financier, Jacques Necker, and the mother of the famous novelist and writer, Madame de Staël) but, when he returned to England, his father decided that this girl's family was too obscure and poor to be united with that of an English gentleman and obliged his son to abandon the relationship. 'After a painful struggle I yielded to my fate; I sighed as a lover, I obeyed as a son' is Gibbon's well-known summary of this episode. When later his father died, he records the event with, 'I submitted to the order of Nature; and my grief was soothed by the conscious satisfaction that I had discharged all the duties of filial piety.'

The manner in which Gibbon records these two significant moments in his life does not suggest that his equilibrium was easily disturbed; but then the effect may be only one of a particular style: of a fondness for balanced antitheses and a constant tendency towards epigrammatic neatness. The most discussed feature of that style is its irony and one consequence of favouring the ironic mode is a feeling in the reader that authors are sounding pleased with themselves. Yet why should people who are looking back on their lives *not* feel that, on the whole, things have turned out satisfactorily? 'I have much to be pleased with', said Joseph Heller, the author of *Catch 22*, 'including myself. I have wanted to succeed and I have.' In 1846, when he was in his mid-seventies,

Wordsworth, for whom being Poet Laureate was clearly not enough, wrote that he often thought his life had been 'in a great measure wasted'. This seems to have been because he had standards set so high, or an egotism so all-consuming, that nothing he had achieved could ever satisfy his expectations. There are many people who, viewed from the outside, have been successful in their professions but whose success has been dependent on a drive and ambition that never stops making them feel they could have done better.

Negotiating between the glass half-full and half-empty is a problem for anyone who is at a point in their life when they feel they need to take stock; and perhaps one of the most striking commentaries on that situation comes from Dr Johnson in the 88th number of his *Idler*:

> We do not indeed so often disappoint others as ourselves. We not only think more highly than others of our own abilities, but allow ourselves to form hopes which we never communicate, and please our thoughts with employments which none will ever allot to us, and with elevations to which we are never expected to rise; and when our days and years have passed away in common business or common amusements, and we find at last that we have suffered our purposes to sleep till the time of action is past, we are reproached only by our own reflections; neither our friends or enemies wonder that we live and die like the rest of mankind; that we live without notice, and die without memorial; they know not what task we had proposed, and therefore cannot discern whether it is finished.

Immediately drawn although I am to a passage like this, and to Johnson's writing in general, I can see that some might find it a little too pessimistic. One of his greatest achievements is 'The Vanity of Human Wishes', an adaptation of a poem by the Latin satirist Juvenal, in which Johnson moves through various different fields of human endeavour in order to demonstrate, with a predictability that becomes almost comic, that they are all likely to end in disappointment and failure.

There is a strange kind of satisfaction, and even pleasure, to be derived from the kind of thinking illustrated in the *Idler* passage, especially for those who are reflecting on how little they themselves have managed to achieve in their lives. Often associated with it is the option people always have of diminishing the value of the success they never had by a change of perspective. 'I dwelt upon the conviction which had long possessed me', writes the nineteenth-century author known as Mark Rutherford, 'that I was *insignificant*, that there was *nothing much in me*. ... And yet there is consolation. The universe is infinite, in the presence of its celestial magnitudes who is there who is really great or small, and what is the difference between you and me, my work and yours?' This would be more genuinely consoling if our awareness of living in a universe that is infinite, and of being a mere speck in the history of Time, were more continuous or vivid than it usually is. A widower with no children, Dr Johnson seems to be concentrating in the passage from *The Idler* on the public realm and discounting the possibility that people can receive all the appreciation they need from their families. Yet, even as regards this public aspect, it is perhaps relevant here to remember that he himself hardly lived without notice and died without memorial. The point he makes is similar to one made by Hobbes in claiming that the only true judge of our value is the public; but he enforces it in a far more seductively eloquent fashion. The lesson is a stern one but to be reminded that we are likely to be very much like 'the rest of mankind', and so eloquently, remains a salutary experience, however much Johnson's words may provide a covert way, different from Rutherford's but no less effective, of letting us off the hook. What I mean is that the ego can be soothed to a limited extent by a demonstration to others, and ourselves, that we not so stupid as to be unaware of our insignificance.

'The first and indispensable requisite of happiness is a clear conscience, unsullied by the reproach or remembrance of an unworthy action', writes Gibbon, who evidently felt that he had nothing to worry about in that department. For many people, however, taking stock means remembering some episodes they would prefer to forget: it involves coming to terms with guilt. This is what is at issue in the third of those 'gifts reserved for age' which are described by the 'familiar compound ghost' the narrator meets in the second section of T.S. Eliot's *Little Gidding*. The first of these gifts is 'the cold friction of expiring sense', which is as fine a brief description of failing physical powers one can imagine. The second is 'the conscious impotence of rage / At human folly', which is recognisable enough, but which the old need to steer clear of as much as possible if they want to live out their last years in tranquillity and not irritate their younger neighbours. However, it is the final, equally cheering gift, that is relevant here:

> And last, the rending pain of re-enactment
> Of all that you have done, and been; the shame
> Of motives late revealed, and the awareness
> Of things ill done and done to others' harm

> *Which once you took for exercise of virtue.*
> *Then fools' approval stings, and honour stains.*

Eliot has a special gift for expressing guilt and these remarkable lines are deservedly celebrated and remembered. It is hard not to recall in reading them the difficult circumstances of his own life and that he had felt obliged, no doubt justifiably, to help commit his first wife to a lunatic asylum. Yet, in other respects, his life was quite extraordinarily successful. Did he then feel stained by all the honours he received and did he regard all those involved in awarding him the Nobel Prize, or giving him the Order of Merit, as fools? The phenomenon he is analysing in these lines is retrospective understanding. Looking back over their lives, individuals can see themselves in certain situations and recognise for the first time the reasons for a role they played in them. Eliot's way of looking at the past makes any harm one might have done unintentional – unaware at the time of the motives one had for certain actions and mistaking them for 'exercise of virtue', whereas the harm that most exercises in retrospection are likely to recover, does not, more commonly, have that excuse.

The early part of Rousseau's *Confessions*, for example, is dominated by an incident in which he stole a silver ribbon from his employer and afterwards blamed the theft on one of the other servants who was then dismissed. One need not have an over-tender conscience to find this action difficult to expiate, especially for someone who had been brought up as Rousseau had in Calvinist Geneva where there were no Catholic priests around to offer absolution. The title of his autobiography is significant and it may be that the disappearance of the confessional plays some minor role in the increasing popularity of the autobiographical form after he had shown the way. Guilt is uncomfortable baggage to carry around, or to deal with at the end of life. The topic clearly interested Shakespeare but his guilty men are usually murderers whose crimes catch up with them, like Richard III or Macbeth, rather than old men taking stock. Someone who corresponds closer to this latter model is that notorious insomniac Henry IV. What keeps him awake at night is anxiety about what will happen to his kingdom once his eldest son and heir takes over; but he is also worried about the 'by-paths and indirect crook'd ways' that allowed him to acquire the kingdom in the first place. As far as those are concerned, he is in a similar position to Claudius who, after the murder of Hamlet's father, feels he cannot be forgiven for his crime while he is still enjoying its benefits. Henry has the idea that the sin he committed in deposing Richard II will be forgotten once he is no more and succeeded by Hal since 'all the soil of the achievement / Goes with me into the earth'; but the serious misgivings he had about his eldest son in the first part of the play surface again at the end of the second, especially when he wakes up to find that Hal has taken away the crown on finding his father asleep and believing him already dead. At that point he has a speech about how 'foolish over-careful fathers' are when they make heroic sacrifices for their children and then discover that they are like bees who come back to the hive laden with honey only to be 'murder'd for our pains'. This Lear-like alarm is seen to be unjustified once Hal reveals himself as a dutiful son, although his military triumphs in France do not in fact dispose of the guilt his father had been feeling. We know this because, in his prayer before Agincourt, Hal, or Henry V as he then is, asks God not to remember at that particular moment 'the fault / My father made in compassing the crown', and describes all the efforts he has made to expiate the family sin including, 'Two chantries, / Where the sad and solemn priests / Sing still for Richard's soul'.

The great nineteenth- and twentieth-century philanthropists who left millions for the establishment of libraries, universities and charitable institutions may have been moved by pure generosity. They may only have wanted to perpetuate their names but it is just possible they also felt that they needed to make amends for how they had managed to become quite so rich in the first place. There are few people who can be as easy about their past behaviour as Gibbon. Many of the poems in Clive James's *Sentenced to Life*, one of the collections published between his first diagnosis of cancer and his death, centre around memories of the past and a recurrent motif in them is guilt. 'My sin was to be faithless', he writes in the opening poem; 'Far too casually / I broke faith when it suited me', he says in 'Leçons des ténèbres'; and in 'Echo Point' there is, 'His body that betrayed you has gone on / To do the same for him.' In 'Rounded with a Sleep', he talks of 'One long finale, soaked through with regret, / Somehow designed to expiate self-blame' and then refers to 'these last years of grief. / As I repent and yet find no relief.' Lines like these might suggest that anguish is a dominant presence in all the poems but this is far from being the case. James is too naturally sanguine and has too much wit to allow that to happen; and his verse has, in addition, a constant tendency towards epigrammatic point. 'Tired out from getting up and getting dressed / I lie down for a while to get some rest', begins his 'Elementary Sonnet'. 'Where there is leisure for fiction there is little grief', Dr Johnson famously remarked of Milton's tribute to a dead friend; and it might equally be said that anyone who takes care that his guilt should be well-expressed cannot be feeling it too strongly. This is the same or at least a similar problem as the one raised by wondering whether Gibbon's ironies mean that he was, in fact, smug. A style that is second nature to writers is not something they can do much about; although how autobiographical writing, and in this case autobiographical confession, is responded to by its readers is in any event a matter out of their authors' control. The lines in an autobiography can never be written so close together without some people feeling that they can read between them.

Unless they are like Gibbon, most old people who review their past honestly are obliged – always supposing their memory is more or less intact! – to acknowledge a certain amount of guilt. Most of them also have to accept more or less public insignificance even if in their retirement speeches they wisely refrain from suggesting that the gap they are about to leave behind is like the hole made in the water by a stick (once it has been taken out). Yet even those who have achieved a degree of fame or recognition have only to apply a little of that perspective Rutherford invokes to see it disappear. 'In old age', Gibbon wrote, 'the consolation of hope is reserved for the tenderness of parents, who commence a new life in their children; the faith of enthusiasts, who sing Hallelujahs above the clouds; and the vanity of authors, who presume the immortality of their name and writings.' Yet, as Gibbon here hints, post-mortem fame can only ever be a *presumption* and all monuments, whether in literature or elsewhere, are 'frail and perishable'. Most humans are ineradicable social beings who want to be well thought of, even when they are dead. Most of them are also reconciled to never being famous but nevertheless feel some anxiety about how they will be thought of after death. They know they are going to be precluded from riding in triumph through Persepolis but hope that the only way they will be remembered is not as the person who had to clean up behind the horses.

'Taking stock' is an image from book-keeping that does not perhaps adequately convey the juggling of pluses and minuses any cool, conscientious exercise in retrospection implies. Insofar as this exercise concerns regrets, Diane Athill has a better one when she says that anyone who looks back on his or her life is bound to see a landscape 'pockmarked' with them; but it is characteristic of her then to attribute the relatively small number she discovers in her own case to 'a preponderance of common-sense over imagination'. Those occasions for regret she has not conveniently forgotten, concern not having had any offspring and they only slide into guilt when she recalls having failed to help a cousin who had been deserted by her husband and left with three small children to look after. Yet she ends her reflections on this topic with, 'I'm not sure that digging out past guilts is a useful occupation for the very old, given that one can do so little about them. I have reached a stage at which one hopes to be forgiven for concentrating on how to get through the present.' The insertion of 'very' here might prompt the thought that Wordsworth was not too wide of the mark when he talked of 'animal *tranquillity*' in relation to his old man travelling, although Athill appears to have been fortunate in avoiding the grosser manifestations of what for that figure was the accompanying decay. Yet to torment oneself over irredeemable past mistakes would indeed seem a waste of that ever-decreasing allotment of time an old person has left.

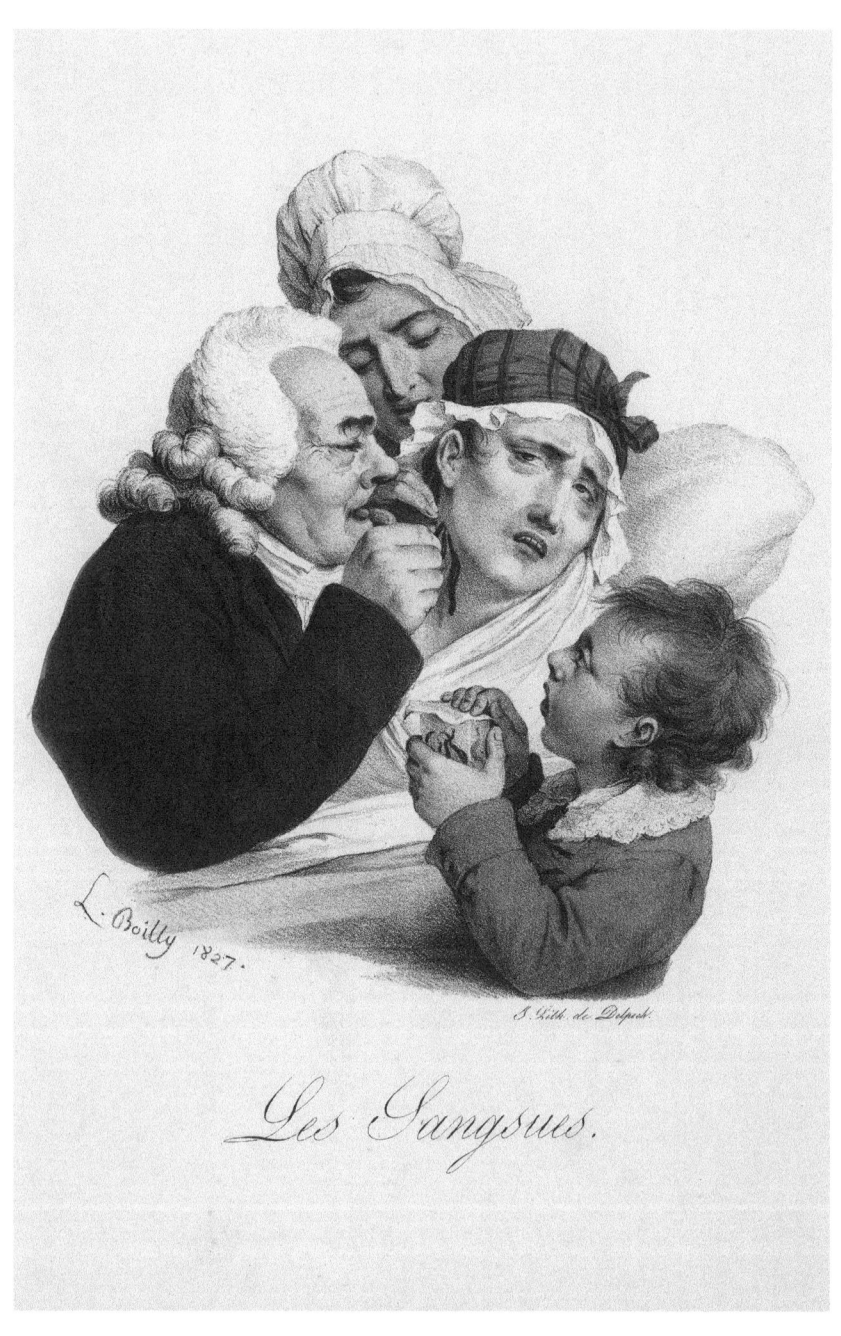

Applying the Leeches
Lithograph by F.S. Delpech from a painting by L. Boily, c. 1827

10

Doctoring and Dying

Although a robust constitution may not do Wordsworth's Michael much good, for most people a happy and contented old age depends on continuing health. Without ever having been robust, this is what Gibbon celebrates in his autobiography or memoir, while Athill's report on health issues is similar to his, although she is more aware that anyone who in this matter is consistently lucky 'beyond their expectations … ends by becoming smug'. What her words again suggest is the significance of temperament, as well as health, in making old age happy, even discounting her own unexpected literary success and celebrity at a time when it would have been reasonable for her to have abandoned all hope of either. It used to be the habit of many of those with literary aspirations to remind themselves that George Eliot did not publish her first novel until she was 40, and then become depressed when they passed that age. That *Stet*, the memoir of Athill's involvement in the publishing trade which brought her a good deal of attention, came out so late in her life suggests to other aspirants rather more breathing time. As the years advanced, she was no more than Gibbon in any danger of being in 'unregarded corners thrown'.

Gibbon and Athill are exceptions. For most people, increasing age means an increasing involvement with the medical profession. In the past this was largely a waste of time (and money) because there was little doctors could do for them, lacking as they did today's detailed scientific understanding of how the body works, what happens when its workings are hampered or arrested, and how certain diseases operate to destroy it. This does not mean that a wealth of expertise was not built up regarding which plants were usefully therapeutic, although a reasonable proportion of those administered probably did as much harm as good, or that even in the literary world there are not records of successful surgical interventions that almost certainly lengthened their subjects' lives. There was Pepys' operation for the removal of a stone from his urinary tract, for example, excellently described by Claire Tomalin in her biography of him or Fanny Burney's mastectomy, equally well recounted by John Wiltshire in his recent book about her. Yet, if doctors in Shakespeare's time had known more, they would not have been so helpless when faced with the plague that closed his theatre so often; and nor would both their predecessors and successors have so often become the satirical targets of writers such as Chaucer, Molière, and very many others. Even in the eighteenth century, when a more rigorous, experimental method was just beginning to take hold, the poet Matthew Prior could write, 'Cur'd yesterday of my disease, / I died last night of my Physician'; and in *Tristram Shandy* Sterne enjoys himself making fun of a ludicrously incompetent obstetrician in Dr Slop. A century later, George Eliot's magnificent portrayal in *Middlemarch* of the unavailing struggles of a reforming doctor called Lydgate illustrates that, in the English provinces at least, custom and superstition remained the order of the day.

Plato believed that the length of any life was predetermined and his fatalism survives in several popular expressions ('it was her time'); but you were lucky in the past if your life was not in the hands of a doctor who, insufficiently aware of how in critical situations there was nothing to be done beyond allowing Nature to take its course, did not shorten it. An illustration of the dangers patients both young and old used to encounter when they consulted the medical profession is its belief in, and reliance on bloodletting as a sovereign remedy for almost all disorders. Dr Johnson was an acute and life-long observer of his own bodily processes and believed that taking copious amounts of blood from his body helped what he called his asthma. That could have been true but in the vast majority of illnesses bloodletting served no useful purpose and could indeed have been counterproductive in that it weakened the body's natural resistance, especially when that body was old.

Before the days of the throwaway syringe, a usual way of drawing blood ('cupping' was the term for it) meant making an incision in the vein with a sharp instrument; but doctors could also use leeches. Of all Wordsworth's poems concerning old men, 'Resolution and Independence' is the one most about himself. It describes how his cheerfulness during a particularly fine morning on the moors is suddenly succeeded by depression and a host of gloomy and self-critical thoughts about the future. How could he expect others to 'Build for him, sow for him, and at his call / Love him, who for himself will take no heed at all?' These reflections are interrupted when he sees a very old man by one of the pools on the moor. At first sight he appears like an integral part of the natural scenery, as did the old man in 'Animal Tranquillity and Decay'; but further inspection reveals someone bent almost double with the weight of years, or with osteoporosis we would probably now say ('feet and head / Coming together in life's pilgrimage'). He seems to be supporting himself on a staff and so represents a traditional symbol of old age, still sometimes seen in road signs indicating that old people might be crossing. However, although the staff may be a means of support, it is also being used to stir the waters of the pool in the old man's search for leeches: '"Once I could meet them on every side, / But they have dwindled long by slow decay; / Yet still I persevere, and find them where I may."'

Wordsworth will take heart from the way the old man talks about his trade and use the fact that he is still able to make some kind of living as a reproach to his own gloomy thoughts; yet it may at first seem that what the leech-gatherer represents, in addition to resolution and independence, is the sadness of those who have spent their life in a certain profession, or in acquiring certain skills, only to find there is no longer much or any call for them, that here we are dealing with that rapid social change which can add to the misfortunes of old age by making people feel useless and stranded. And yet the application of leeches, and blood-letting generally, remained a very popular treatment throughout the nineteenth century, and even up to the First World War. Not long after Wordsworth wrote about his leech-gatherer, Byron went to Greece and developed what was described as a 'fever'. A thorough sceptic as far as phlebotomy was concerned, he became too weak to resist his doctors who prescribed copious blood-letting, although not necessarily with leeches. This was perhaps in the mistaken belief that they could thereby evacuate the noxious elements that had taken hold of their patient's body. The origins of Byron's difficulties were almost certainly malarial, and he had suffered periodically from them before. After a particularly bad bout in Venice, he was able to congratulate himself that he had recovered without any intervention from the medical profession but, since he had taken his own personal doctor with him to Greece, there was no avoiding it in this final episode. He might have died of his fever whatever his doctors did; but there is general agreement that their treatment almost certainly reduced rather than increased his chances of survival.

That progress in medicine was initially slow is illustrated by what happened with tuberculosis. The discovery of the bacillus at the root of the trouble dates from the early 1880s but an effective method for combatting it was not available until after the Second World War. One of the very many victims of the disease was George Orwell. He had a rich friend who had heard about exciting new developments in the United States and was able to secure samples of streptomycin in the late 1940s, but because it was not known how best to administer the drug, it made Orwell increasingly sick rather than better and he died before the problems were worked out. It could be said that his was a position we all now occupy, however long we live. That is to say that advances in medicine are today so frequent that it is almost certain there would be a cure, or at least a palliative, for whatever kills us, were we able to live long enough to see it. One aspect of the situation this creates is ironically referred to in 'Cure' by the Romanian poet Marin Sorescu when he says, 'When the cure of a disease is discovered / Those who have died of the illness / Ought to rise again / And go on living / Until they fall sick with another disease / Whose cure has not yet been discovered'. Although any hint of poetry has disappeared in the translation, the thought is apposite and witty and therefore thoroughly deserving of inclusion in D.J. Enright's *Faber Book of Fevers and Frets*.

Throughout the ages, and well into our own time, the relative absence of genuinely effective medicine has always favoured bogus treatments. When Volpone is trying to seduce the young wife of one of his gulls, he disguises himself as a famous mountebank and sets up a stall outside her house selling an oil that will cure every kind of illness, as well as keeping those who take it young. Four centuries later, in what is perhaps the best of his novels (*Tono-Bungay*), H.G. Wells describes how the hero's uncle makes a fortune selling a tonic the putative powers of which are similar to Volpone's oil. Valuing Wells for reasons much like those of Cummings, Lawrence particularly admired *Tono-Bungay* but that did not prevent him, when his 'chest problems' showed no signs of abating, from yielding to pressure from his family and taking a 'patent medicine' that went by the extraordinary name of Umckaloabo. This was the invention of a certain Major Stevens who was the founder of the 'Consumption Cure Company', and thought by some to be the model for the uncle in Wells' novel. When Lawrence was finally dying of tuberculosis in a sanatorium in the south of France, he was visited by Wells who was wealthy enough to have provided himself with a second home in the nearby town of Grasse. Three years before, Lawrence had read the first volume of his visitor's heavily autobiographical 'novel', *The World of William Clissold*, and been deeply disappointed. It seems to have made an impression on him similar to the one Gibbon made on Cummings since, in his review, Lawrence identified in the book a note of elderly self-satisfaction, typical of old people inclined to attribute any success they have had in life entirely to their own efforts. After returning from the sanatorium, Wells reported that the much younger man's illness was chiefly a matter of hysteria, a diagnosis Lawrence was able to refute by dying less than a month later.

It may be a mite premature to echo one of the doctors in Molière's *Le Malade Imaginaire* and say that these days, with so many clinically tested drugs on the market, and effective treatment available for diseases and disorders that in the past made old age a rarity, situations like those of Orwell and Lawrence are unlikely to arise and that 'we have changed all that'. Yet although Athill herself remained healthy late in life, she gives a harrowing account of having to care for a former lover as he suffered the misdiagnoses, delays and inadequate treatment of the British national health service. The pressure that service was already under (massively increased recently by the Covid pandemic) was suggested by Enright in a short poem he wrote about a visit to his doctor. 'GP' it is called and begins, 'General paralysis of the features', in order to indicate how unenthusiastic the doctor seems at the author's arrival in the consulting room.[1] After listening to an account of his symptoms, the doctor lists a number of reasons why it would be inappropriate to prescribe painkillers and then asks to be reminded of the patient's age ('as if he didn't know'):

> *You are a number, a number of years,*
> *And there lie diagnosis and prognosis too.*

As Enright understands, it can be hard to garner sympathy for illness and suffering in old age because, as people are inclined to indicate, they come with the territory and is what we all have to expect. Being old is, as Bette Davis is supposed to have said, 'No place for sissies.' Nothing could be more reasonable than that doctors should be more concerned with disorders in young lives than in those where the lifespan is nearing its end. Yet that does not make being on the wrong end of this equation less uncomfortable as Enright makes clear with some asperity when he writes:

> *Poor fellow, he's so bored. Cheer up*
> *You want to tell him, there are hordes*
> *Of hardy kids in the waiting room,*
> *One has just thrown up on your magazines.*

---

1. The poem is included in his collection, *Old Men and Comets*.

Nothing is yet perfect in medical treatment, nor in the relationship between doctors and their patients, yet the difference from only fifty years ago is staggering. This is clear from a poem in Clive James' collection, *Injury Time*, entitled 'Ibrutinib'. Those who have picked up a prescription from the chemists recently will recognise in this word a collocation of syllables so barbarous and unnatural that it becomes impossible to remember. Ibrutinib is in fact a drug recently developed, as James expresses it in his poem, 'To put the kibosh on your CLL', or chronic lymphocytic leukaemia. He jauntily imagines it as an army platoon fighting the Viet Cong in the jungle: 'let's see what Ibrutinib can do / To win the war whose battlefield is you.' Unless the drug can do its job, James concludes, 'things might tend / To go bananas in a serious way. / But not yet. Down the hatch. This is today.' The comparison with the Vietnam war may not suggest much optimism in the long term, but that the drug has been effective up to a point is proved by the presence of the poem itself.

The wonders of modern medicine can only delay but never prevent the inevitable. As Justice Shallow says, after Silence has remarked that they are both due to follow all their former acquaintances who are now dead: 'Certain, 'tis certain; very sure, very sure. Death, as the Psalmist saith, is certain to all; all shall die', although he then adds immediately, 'How a good yoke of bullocks at Stamford fair?' We are all going to die but a crucial question is quite when. Near the start of *Remembrance of Things Past*, the narrator describes his old aunt who has taken to her bed and managed to discourage two kinds of potential visitors. The first of these urges her to try to get up and points out how much she would benefit from a little fresh air, while the second takes her complaints seriously and has a disturbing tendency to agree that she is in a bad way. The only visitor she can tolerate is the one who, when the aunt insists the end is near, always replies, 'Knowing your trouble as well as you yourself do, Madame Octave, I'm sure you'll live to be a hundred'; but this does not completely please the old lady because, as Proust says, she prefers not to have 'assigned to her years a precise end'.

In his final years, Simon Gray, author of perhaps the first and certainly the best play about teaching English in a university (*Butley*), wrote a series of 'smoking diaries'. Their title refers to the habit he found impossible to give up and which would lead to his death. In the course of these brilliant books, Gray describes the difficulties and irritations of relations with the various doctors he was obliged to consult as his lung cancer worsened. Writers are in some ways powerful people, their ability effectively to represent the world giving them a control of it that the less articulate lack, but if so many of them in the past have satirised doctors, it may partly be because of a power struggle in which they have more than met their match, irrespective of what happens to be the current state of medical knowledge. After all, what is at stake in their encounters with the medical profession matters so much more to one party than to the other.

In the last of his diaries, which is called *Coda*, there is a doctor Gray especially disliked to whom he gives the name of Dr Rootle. He had reached the stage when it was crucial to decide, via an operation, whether the lump on his neck was a new cancer that it was right to treat separately, or a sign that the cancer cells were in the blood and that therefore palliative care was all that would be possible. Dr Rootle asks whether, in the case of this second outcome (which he clearly thought the more likely), Gray would like a prognosis. 'No', replies his wife firmly, who was present with her husband, but Gray himself, confused by all this talk of a prognosis before the diagnosis the operation would bring, begins to ask 'How long …?' His intention is to enquire how long, after the operation was over, he would have to wait to be told the results but his words are taken to mean how long it would be, should those results be unfavourable, before he died. 'About a year', says Dr Rootle, from the side of his mouth but 'loud and clear', and with an expression on his face that, while befittingly calm and solemn, conveyed a certain satisfaction: 'Mission accomplished! Difficult deed done, and out of the side of my mouth too!' 'But I didn't ask that question, so kindly withdraw your answer', Gray remembers feeling, wanting not only to curse the doctor as profanely as he could, but also to kill him so that he could say, as he plunged the knife in, 'That's a year longer than you have, matey':

> The thing I think I understood immediately, before I'd even thought about it, was that a doctor who tells you that you have a year to live has taken the year away from you – from the moment the sentence was delivered – the knowledge would never be cleared from my consciousness, the last thought at night, the first in the morning, for the rest of my life.

It is clear from Gray's response to his doctor's prognosis why even the idea she might live to be 100 can make Proust's old aunt feel uncomfortable. Aunt Léonie is like the father of Emma Woodhouse in having chosen what one might call the valetudinarian option. This consists in hunkering down, not exposing oneself to places where death might be lurking and conserving vital energy. Balzac is unusual among great writers in having spent a long period writing what would now be considered trash before entering the mainstream and being taken seriously. The first novel to mark his breakthrough is called *La Peau de chagrin*, which is usually translated in English as 'The Wild Ass's Skin'. It tells of a young man, at the end of his tether, who wanders into an antiques shop where he finds an old piece of untanned leather that turns out to have magical properties similar to Aladdin's lamp. Every time he makes a wish it is granted and he is thus able to access all the wine, women and song he had previously been too poor to enjoy. The difference from Aladdin's lamp is that the wild ass's skin is an indication of how long he will live and shrinks a little every time one of his wishes is fulfilled (the underlying notion is similar to those Balzac entertained on the link between sex and creativity). Proust's aunt and Mr Woodhouse live their lives as if they had this piece of leather in sight all the time, but there is another strategy for dealing with approaching death that consists in making the most of the time that is left. 'See Naples and die', it used to be said, but these days that is only one of numerous great cities on the itineraries of the old. In *About Time*, Irma Kurtz describes well what life is like on a cruise ship full of old people, rich enough to prefer sea travel to expensive sheltered housing or a care home, and able to visit many more famous places than Naples. All this is with a doctor on board who deals discreetly with the one or two deaths that inevitably occur during the boat's passage. As an option, this is perhaps better than sitting at home waiting for death to arrive, but it does depend not only on the continuation of reasonable health but also the right mental state. It is a custom in many countries to allow a condemned criminal to order any food he or she likes on the night before execution. Yet it would take a special nature – something like that of Shakespeare's prisoner Banardine in his *Measure for Measure* – to tuck cheerfully into Beef Wellington, or Duck *á l'orange*, just before being hanged or having your head chopped off.

There are lots of death scenes in literature but, for obvious reasons, not many descriptions of what it is actually like to die. Amongst the most famous of the latter is Tolstoy's *The Death of Ivan Ilyich*. This is only a novella, or long short story, but so deeply imagined that the reader becomes anxious for it to stop along with its protagonist's sufferings. The story begins after Ivan Ilyich is dead and describes the relief his family feel that it is all over, and the speculations of his colleagues at the magistrate courts as to what his disappearance means for their hopes of promotion. It then relates how he became a successful lawyer by always doing what was more or less the right, conventional thing and extended those habits into his private life. Comfortably off, even though his family's expectations had always had a tendency to outrun his income, he had moved to a new house. There, he bruises his lower abdomen while making some alterations. This gives rise to a pain which afterwards never leaves him, even though he consults several doctors who only ever pretend that they can improve the situation. As his illness develops, so does his alienation from his wife, children, colleagues and the world in general. There are uncomfortable details of the progress of his disease and Tolstoy does not shrink from describing the humiliating incontinence that accompanies Ivan Ilyich's last weeks. Religion in the formal sense is shown to be of little or no help but in the two hours before his death, after three days of what is described as screaming pain, there is a glimmer of hope as Ivan is suddenly able to break out of his egotism and feel sympathy for his wife and daughter while they are witnessing his suffering. This means that he experiences both release and relief in his last moments.

There is no final glimmer in a novella sometimes thought to have been partly inspired by *The Death of Ivan Ilyich* and written by Tolstoy's compatriot, Chekhov. This is in some ways more relevant here because its protagonist, Nikolai Stepanovich, is elderly, whereas Ivan Ilyich is only in his mid-forties when he dies. Unlike Ivan, Nikolai has no need to consult doctors because he himself already is one, a distinguished and celebrated specialist who lectures on medicine at the university. He can recognise the symptoms of problems with his heart that mean he has not long to live, just as Chekhov's own medical training would have allowed him to track the tuberculosis from which he suffered. Similar to Ivan's case is that the professor's illness causes him to become even more alienated from the interests of his wife and children than he was before. The only young person whose company he enjoys is his ward Katya, who is the daughter of a colleague but has been brought up in his own home from the age of seven after being orphaned. In adolescence, this girl has decided that she wanted to become an actress, gone off to join a theatre group elsewhere in Russia, fallen in love with an actor and then had an illegitimate child before being abandoned by him. Returning to her home town, and using the money she has inherited from her dead parents to set up house there, Katya is something of marked woman and outsider, but the dying professor finds comfort in going to talk to her. On one of the occasions Chekhov dramatises, the two of them are interrupted by another member of the university who admires Katya and leads her into a conversation in which they both decry the world around them and, in particular, the university where, in their opinion, there has been a sharp deterioration of quality in both students and staff. The professor is upset by the tone of these exchanges and protests against their acrid cynicism, and yet his own view of the world around him is similarly harsh and disillusioned, coloured like that of Ivan Ilyich, or of Anna Karenina on her way to commit suicide at the railway station, by a feeling that everything is ugly and drab, and nothing is worthwhile. The climax of the story comes when Katya, who is increasingly unhappy and desperate, comes to ask him for advice on the best means of escaping from the hopelessness of her life. That, fond as he is of her, there is nothing he feels he can offer means that, although Chekhov's novella is much less harrowing than Tolstoy's, it is in some ways more depressing and justifies the title by which it usually appears in English, *A Dreary Story*.

Chekhov does not describe what it feels like to die, the difficulty of which is obviously that there can be no recourse to personal experience, only what it is to know you are dying, but he is close to Tolstoy in his depiction of how this knowledge can affect someone's personal relationships and view of life in general. It is as if their two protagonists had been brought to subscribe to Pascal's powerful vision of a world in which everyone spends their time distracting themselves from the true misery and meaninglessness of their state. Chekhov hints that this mood, this depression we might now say, is one of the physical consequences of illness, but it can also be one of the consequences of ageing. A service the social sciences could usefully perform would be to calculate how many more misanthropes there are after the age of 70 than before.

When Jean Améry went to hear Jean-Paul Sartre, that 'god of his youth', lecture, he noted how Sartre preferred to speak to young people because 'the future has always been for him the true dimension of humanity' despising as he does 'the search for lost time as much as the Romantics' erotization of death'. As Chekhov's professor illustrates, however, life can become difficult when there is no longer much future available and when that God, whom Pascal thought of as the solution to man's misery, is for most people not present on the horizon either. Some version of Sartre's attitude does, nevertheless, seem to be one of the best methods the old can adopt for warding off depression and apathy. In a chapter in his autobiography entitled 'Pros and Cons of Reaching Ninety', Bertrand Russell confessed that as a young man he believed that when he reached old age he would 'retire from the world and live a life of elegant culture, reading all the great books that [he] ought to have read at an earlier date.' Yet a feeling that his own country was led by 'men without imagination and without capacity for adaptation in the world', together with the threat of nuclear annihilation, had kept him unable 'to acquiesce patiently in what was happening' and made him continue working for a safer future. It was presumably this looking forward rather than back that made his old age more bearable. 'Keep on the sunny side, always on the sunny side' is the refrain of one of the country and western classics, but perhaps more effective would be the injunction to be more interested in the future than the past, however little of that commodity is likely to be personally available.

The Death of Addison
Painting by S.W. Reynolds the Younger (1794-1872).

11

Ending Up

In former times, the death to which we are all heading was much more of a public event and the air of theatricality often surrounding a deathbed encouraged the tradition (or myth) of famous last words. These were thought to carry a special authority because of the circumstances in which they were spoken. As Shakespeare's John of Gaunt, in *Richard II*, puts it:

O, but they say the tongues of dying men
Inforce attention like deep harmony.
Where words are scarce, they are seldom spent in vain,
For they breathe truth that breathe their words in pain.

An astonishing indication of the potency of this tradition occurs in Dr Johnson's short biography of one of the founders of modern journalism, Joseph Addison.[1] He was concerned about his stepson, Edward Rich, the seventh Earl of Warwick, a young man of 'very irregular life, and perhaps of loose opinions'. He therefore summoned him to his bedside in order to witness, Johnson writes, 'how a Christian can die'. It is difficult to read this account without hearing a faint echo of irony in the background. This is not because of any scepticism in Johnson's approach to Christianity but should rather be attributed to the fearful feelings that the prospect of death aroused in him. In theory, the last person who should fear death is a Christian as devout as he was; but this is to ignore that last judgement which was such a favourite subject for Renaissance painters,

---

1. In Johnson's *Lives of the Poets*.

with blessed souls ascending to Heaven and sinners cast down into the other place. Johnson had too much concern about being among the latter to anticipate death with anything but grave anxiety.

Not everyone felt quite the same about the final reckoning as he did. Dr Johnson died in 1784 and it was less than 50 years later that Byron published his satirical *Vision of Judgement* (1822). The occasion was the death of an old and sick George III, which had been greeted with what he considered odious sycophancy in a work by the poet laureate, Robert Southey. Byron's response to Southey's original *Vision of Judgement* was to give a hilariously burlesque account of the animated discussions at Heaven's gate as to whether or not the old king should be let in. He arrives there closely followed by Satan and then the Archangel Michael. While these two talk over George's case together, Byron works up the character of St Peter who is grumpy and bored but roused to comic indignation when Satan, who is, of course, arguing against the late king's admittance to heaven, points out that he had opposed Catholic emancipation, thereby oppressing the very people most likely to revere Peter's own sainthood. 'Ere Heaven shall ope her portals to this Guelf, / While I am guard, may I be damn'd myself!', Peter exclaims. Byron admits that he is in no position to believe himself exempt from judgement, and that he is therefore 'not a whit more difficult to damn, / Than is to land a late-hooked fish', but in a period when Satan would be newly declared the hero of Milton's *Paradise Lost*, Byron is concerned to prevent his political enemies from using the last judgement as a means of both propaganda and intimidation. One of the strengths of his poem is that he is able to bring out the absurdity of making too much fuss over the death of an old and sick man while at the same time not suggesting that what he himself feels is vengeful glee.

Almost any literary student who hears the words 'vision of judgement' these days is likely to think of Byron rather than Southey, the parody having replaced the original. A similar fate overtook one of Southey's other poems more specifically concerned with old age. This is called 'The Old Man's Comforts and How He Gained Them' and begins with a youth asking 'Father William' how he has managed to remain so hale and hearty. He explains that when he himself was young he took care not to abuse his health, always remembering that he would not be young for ever, and that, if he now remains cheerful, it is because: 'In the days of my youth I remembered my God! / And He hath not forgotten my age.' Although what the old man says may come a little too late in the day for some of us, his implied advice for enjoying a healthy and satisfying last phase is sensible enough; but it clearly irritated Lewis Carroll sufficiently to prompt a version of the original poem, which is now what most people remember, and with considerable pleasure, once the words 'Father William' are pronounced. The youth who is asking in Southey's poem how it is that the old man looks so well has become his son in Lewis Carroll's, and is enquiring why his white-haired father 'incessantly stand[s] on his head – / Do you think, at your age, it is right?' Instead of being lectured on the importance of remembering that he will not always be young, this Father William replies to the question by saying that he once feared headstands might 'injure the brain' but 'now that I'm perfectly sure I have none, / Why, I do it again and again.' Perhaps there is something incorrigible in human nature that makes people prefer a mild joke to sound but dull advice, although a lot does depend on the tone in which the advice is delivered.

Southey's Father William is described as loving to converse cheerfully on death. This was not Dr Johnson's case and his references to it illustrate that even someone as gifted and intelligent as he was could entertain highly contradictory ideas on the subject. He may, on the one hand, have dreaded the idea of judgement but at the same time he had a horror of what he called annihilation, or absence of consciousness. In this he seems to have belonged to a minority. Most of us are not so much frightened of death as the process of dying and are like Woody Allen who has said that he would not mind his own death as long as he wasn't there when it happened.[2] In a conversation that Boswell describes as having taken place on 15 April 1778, Johnson's friend Anna Seward tried to reason him out of his fear by suggesting that it was absurd to dread annihilation when it was 'only a pleasing sleep without a dream'. How could he be anxious about a state of which, by definition, he would not be aware? Johnson replied that the state in question was 'neither pleasing, nor sleep, it is nothing' and then added, somewhat illogically but also understandably, 'mere existence is so much better than nothing, that one would rather exist even in pain than not exist'. A more recent writer who shared this horror of non-existence was Philip Larkin. His poem 'Aubade' is an eloquent protest against 'no sight, no sound, / No touch or taste or smell, nothing to think with, / Nothing to love or link with, / The anaesthetic from which none come round'; and it was Larkin who told his friend Kingsley Amis, 'I am not so much afraid of dying. I am afraid of being dead.' The distinction is an important one, which is not rendered redundant for everybody by Lucretius' well-known observation that, if we are undisturbed by the idea that we did not exist

---

2. In his *Without Feathers* (New York: Ballantine Books, 1983).

before we were born, we have no reason to worry about being in the same non-state after we have gone.

There is a clear rejection of the Lucretian view, traced back as it often is to Epicurus, in the second stanza of another well-known poem by Larkin, more explicitly concerned with old age than 'Aubade'. 'The Old Fools' appears to have been the result of having visited hospital wards for the elderly and has a powerful first stanza in which Larkin inveighs against the old for allowing themselves to be in such a deplorable state – forgetful, drooling from an open mouth, pissing themselves – without screaming in protest. In the second stanza, which is about the final breakup of the body on death, and the nothingness that ensues, he confronts directly the consolation Lucretius offers. 'It's only oblivion', he writes, that we had before but 'then it was going to end, / And was all the time merging with a unique endeavour / To bring to bloom the million-petalled flower / Of being here.' This is a strangely incongruous, romantic image for Larkin whom it is hard to imagine thinking of his life as a university librarian in Hull as a 'million-petalled flower', but the logical point is well taken. There is a difference between a nothingness that we know must have come to an end and one that, for those with no belief in an afterlife, and following what Larkin calls 'the whole hideous, inverted childhood' of old age, goes on for ever.

There are no famous last words associated with Larkin, and the closer one comes to our own time the less likely those that have been recorded are to be authentic. This is because the drugs used to ease a passage out of this world put the dying individual in a state where any kind of coherence becomes impossible. What we particularly like to hear are last words that seem eminently in character. It would be disappointing, for example, if Oscar Wilde had not said, as he was dying in a badly decorated Paris hotel room, that either the wallpaper he was looking at would have to go or he would; and it seems altogether appropriate that Heinrich Heine's last words should have been that God would forgive him because that was after all the business he was in (*c'est son métier*).[3] Yet it is more credible that, just before he died, D.H. Lawrence should have said, 'Wind my watch', since this was an action one can assume he had the habit of taking every evening in a manner that had become quasi-automatic. Lawrence had his own favourite last words, which were associated with Katherine Mansfield, a former close friend and also, like him, a sufferer from tuberculosis. She had tried a number of bogus

---

3. Heine's remark is recorded by Freud in his book on jokes.

cures and spent her final days in an institute in Fontainebleau, run by an Armenian mystic called Gurdjieff, part of whose treatment was to house his patients above a cowshed in a belief that the rising effluvia had a restorative effect. Mansfield's husband, John Middleton Murry, had published in England a moving account of his last meeting with his wife before her death, which Lawrence claimed was all wrong. When Murry had in fact turned up at 'that crank's institute' and asked to see Katherine, Lawrence insisted her last words had been, 'Keep that bugger away from me.'

Lawrence's relish for this final declaration needs some explanation. Murry had been one of his intimate friends (and a supposed model for Gerald in *Women in Love*); but they had numerous quarrels and what particularly soured their relationship was Lawrence's suspicion that Murry had slept with his wife Frieda during the time when, in the 1920s, she had briefly separated from her husband and travelled back to Europe from America without him. One of his responses was a bizarre story he published after he and Frieda had been reunited called 'The Border-Line'. This features a man whose description makes him seem very like Murry about to sleep with a woman who appears very much like Frieda when the ghost of the latter's former husband suddenly appears and hauls the Murry figure out of the bed. By lying on top of his rival, the dead husband provokes in him a tubercular haemorrhage before then making love to his former wife in a mysterious manner that does not involve penetration. Whatever the other significances of this very strange story, it was clearly meant to function rather as Casaubon's will was and to discourage another man from taking up with its author's widow. In that context, it was equally unsuccessful in that, almost as soon as Lawrence was dead, Murry rushed over to the South of France to enjoy a brief affair with Frieda.

The conditions that cast doubt on the authenticity of famous last words do not always pertain. Cicero compares the death of the young to a fierce flame being extinguished by water but says that, when the old die, it is as if 'a spent fire goes out of its own accord'. In an indication that the analogy with apples was around long before D.H. Lawrence came to use it, Cicero goes on:

> Or, as apples, if unripe, are violently wrenched from the tree, while, mature and ripened, they fall, so force takes life from the young, ripeness from the old; and this ripeness of old age is to me so pleasant, that, in proportion as I draw near to

death, I seem to see land, and after a long voyage to be on the point of entering the harbour.[4]

In the peacefulness of this last image, there is no hint of the 'polypathology' which de Beauvoir says usually afflicts the old in the final phase of their lives; and nor of that anxiety about being redundant that those who are spending their last years in retirement can often feel. Yet there are also many who, in these days of State and private pensions, look forward eagerly to the day when they will no longer have to work and welcome it with open arms when it does arrive, as Lamb's superannuated man does. Not to have to get up at a set time every morning, to be no longer under someone else's control, to do more or less as one likes, or to decide to do nothing at all and practise what Karl Marx's son-in-law, Paul Lafargue, championed as *The Right to Be Lazy* because, as Charles de Saint-Évremond said, 'sloth is not without its charms' – these are benefits of the modern world to which thousands and perhaps millions look forward and then enjoy with uncomplicated pleasure. They can be open also to those who have had to give up status and power. In a review of the letters of Horace Walpole to Sir Robert Mann, Macauley describes the political downfall of Carteret, a minister in the reign of George III.[5] After being driven from office, Carteret made a bold and indeed desperate attempt to recover his position and, when that failed, 'retired laughing to his books and his bottle. No statesman ever enjoyed success with so exquisite a relish, or submitted to defeat with so genuine and unforced a cheerfulness.' Ill as he had been used, Horace Walpole reported, he did not seem to have any resentment, or any feeling except thirst. The only hesitation one might have about accepting this account as a model of how best to handle the approach of death is that it seems to imply a possible hastening along the road with large amounts of alcohol, very large amounts if one were to heed the example of *The Old Devils*, Kingsley Amis's novel about the uncomfortable reunion of old friends in Wales. They sometimes remind one of Montaigne's remarks in his essay on vanity that: 'If we were always progressing towards improvement, to be old would be a beautiful thing. But it is a drunkard's progress, formless, staggering, like reeds which the wind shakes as it fancies, haphazardly.'

The problem is that very many human beings are so conditioned that they like to feel useful, and that can be difficult when they no longer have any obvious social function. Of course, a great deal depends on what

---

4. Marcus Tullius Cicero, *Treatises on Friendship and Old Age.*
5. See his *Reviews, Essays and Poems.*

that function has been. Successful politicians like Carteret, or those who have been famous for their sporting achievements, might clearly have more problems in adapting than anyone who has worked on the assembly line, or held a minor clerical position in an office. Away from the world of work, there is the dilemma of those whose concentration had been on attracting members of the opposite sex, like Balzac's Baron Hulot or Lady Wishfort and many of her predecessors in Restoration drama. In his 'Epistle to a Lady', only a few years after Congreve's death, Pope passed a characteristically sharp and unsympathetic judgement on the female members of this group:

> *At last, to follies Youth could scarce defend,*
> *'Tis half their Age's prudence to pretend;*
> *Ashamed to own they gave delight before,*
> *Reduc'd to feign it, when they give no more:*
> *As Hags hold Sabbaths, less for joy than spight,*
> *So these their merry, miserable Night;*
> *Still round and round the Ghosts of Beauty glide,*
> *And haunt the places where their Honour dy'd.*

Lines such as these pose a dilemma familiar to readers of Pope: shock at their malice and admiration for their wonderful point and skill. Most memorable is the final couplet, which those who are inclined to revisit the corridors of a business or institution where they once worked might well be tempted to repeat to themselves, even if they could never have pretended to anything that would be described as beauty, and no particular loss of honour was ever involved. The danger of becoming like a ghost haunting the scenes of one's more youthful activities is why some make the break with a former workplace definitive when they retire and accept that, as they grow old, they increasingly belong to a different caste or race.

One of the many, additional dangers of old age is a certain world-weariness, which was once unusually expressed by François Mauriac in his *Mémoires intérieurs* in relation to the reading of novels. When he was young, he said, novels gave substance to his as yet half-hidden future and revealed to him his own possibilities. As the years passed, however, the characters in fiction no longer found in him sufficient freedom of movement. Having previously lived in the hopes of his youth, what purely fictive creatures could now, with what had been his future more or less decided, spread their wings in such thin air? What he appears to be talking about is one of the negative effects of experience, supplementary to those suggested by Swift, or illustrated by Shakespeare in Polonius. The latter's appearances on stage usually give an entirely different impression of old age from Cicero's, while the harsh manner in which Hamlet responds to the discovery that he has accidently killed the old counsellor ('lug the guts into the neighbour room') is a reminder of how little sympathy the elderly ought to expect in comparison with the feelings associated with the death of someone such as Ophelia, who had all her life before her.

An even greater contrast between the picture of old age drawn by Cicero and the one Shakespeare provides in Polonius can be found in the work of Samuel Beckett. Winnie, who is virtually the only character in the ironically entitled *Happy Days*, is an ageing woman who shows a dogged concern for making sure she looks presentable, even though in the first part of the play she is buried up to her waist in dirt and, in the second, up to her neck; but it is in *Endgame* that the focus is more clearly on what it is like to be old. Nagg, identified as the 'progenitor' of the main character in this play, lives in a dustbin at the back of the stage, alongside his partner Nell who is similarly accommodated. The conditions of their living are illustrated on their first appearance in a series of very short exchanges, which begin as they make a failed attempt to lean towards each other in order to kiss and Nell complains 'Why this farce, day after day?':

> **NAGG:** Can you see me?
> **NELL:** Hardly. And you?
> **NAGG:** What?
> **NELL:** Can you see me?
> **NAGG:** Hardly.
> **NELL:** So much the better, so much the better.
> **NAGG:** Don't say that. [Pause.] Our sight has failed.
> **NELL:** Yes.
>   [Pause. They turn away from each other.]
> **NAGG:** Can you hear me?
> **NELL:** Yes. And you?
> **NAGG:** Yes. [Pause.] Our hearing hasn't failed.
> **NELL:** Our what?

In the final exchange here there is an echo of that exploitation of deafness for comic purposes that I identified in *Volpone*, and there is indeed a grim humour in the sequence as a whole. The total effect is hardly comic, however, or only for those young and buoyant enough to ignore or be unaware of its implications. What one can say is that at least Beckett does not make a special target of old age in that his pessimism extends to the human condition as a whole. We know that he always valued a distinction between two pre-Socratic philosophers, Democritus and Heraclitus, which is conveniently described in one of Montaigne's essays. Both of these men, Montaigne writes, found our human circumstances 'vain and ridiculous' but, whereas this made Heraclitus feel so much compassion that he always wore a sad expression, Democritus 'never went out without a laughing and mocking look on his face'. In the view of Montaigne, usually regarded as an essentially benign figure, this second attitude is preferable, not on account of its being 'more agreeable to laugh than to weep', but because it seemed to him that, 'according to our deserts, we can never be despised enough'.

Beckett was clearly a partisan of the Democritean view and yet, although the world in which Nagg and Nell are reduced to living is so uninviting, and they are clearly afflicted with de Beauvoir's 'polypathology', they do at least have each other. In *Happy Days*, Winnie, whose concern for appearances seems to be regarded by Beckett as typically female and can perhaps be heard also in Nell's 'So much the better, so much the better' in the lines above, has a male companion called Willie to whom she gives the impression of being attached, although he is virtually moribund and scarcely has a line to say. The far from comfortable condition of the two tramps in *Waiting for Godot* is alleviated by their fondness for each other and, like Nagg and Nell or Winnie and Willie, they enjoy short, nostalgic memories of a happier past. It is impossible to say quite how old these tramps are but they are clearly no longer young. Towards the beginning of *Waiting for Godot*, one of them remembers how they had once thought of ending it all by jumping hand in hand off the top of the Eiffel Tower, but that now they are so dishevelled, 'they wouldn't even let us up'. This is a remark that one can imagine one old person with a literary background making to another in a care home; although perhaps more apt would be the question Nagg addresses to Nell in an exchange shortly after those I have just quoted: 'Has he changed your sawdust?'

What Beckett has to say or imply about old age may seem to strike too sombre a note, in spite of its dark comedy, when there are many other, more inspiring models on offer apart from his, or indeed Shakespeare's Lear (whose experiences on the heath have such an obvious influence on *Waiting for Godot*). Moreover, although I may, in discussing various manifestations of that strange desire for post-mortem power or influence, have implied that all it ever represents is a misplaced egotism, that is clearly not the case. In direct contrast, for example, to Browning's bishop ordering his tomb might be elderly campaigners for climate change who know perfectly well they will not be alive to see whether or not their efforts have been crowned with success. Both they and the bishop are, as it were, working in the dark but from very different motives. It is true that these campaigners often say that what they are doing is for their children and grandchildren who could be regarded as in some sense extensions of the self; yet there must be amongst them those who are childless and who therefore represent examples of an altruism that needs no qualifications. They may be counting on what for them is a non-existent future, but for reasons quite different from the pharaohs.

Old age does not always correspond to a traditional stereotype of being selfish, miserable, tight-fisted, out of touch or timid; and yet its essential conditions do not change and the vast majority of us would find as much difficulty as the old man in Chaucer's 'Pardoner's Tale' in finding someone willing to exchange it for youth. It is because he is unsuccessful in this endeavour that he is obliged to continue to walk the earth like a 'restless caityf':

> *And on the ground, which is my modre's gate,*
> *I knokke with my staff, bothe erly and late,*
> *And seye, 'leve [dear] moder, leet me in!*
> *Lo, how I vanish! Flesh, and blood, and skin!'*

The danger in acknowledging these unchanging conditions is to feel angry, envious and resentful, or succumb to self-pity, since this would be to kick against the pricks and forget what a large degree of luck there is in being old at all. Of course, the individual's situation can be transformed by religion yet, in spite of Addison, it is surprising how little difference religion can make to true believers like Johnson, or how insignificant it can be made to seem in the more pessimistic reflections of major characters in Shakespeare, even at a time when religion permeated every aspect of social and private life. What, after all, is recognisably Christian in Hamlet's, 'For in that sleep of death what dreams may come?' Yet there are counter-examples. D.H. Lawrence had an older brother called Ernest who was regarded as the most talented member of the family. When he was embarked on what looked like being a successful business career, he suddenly fell ill and died. The impact on his mother was devastating and she later told her younger son's girlfriend, Jessie Chambers, that she looked forward more to meeting Ernest in Heaven than Jesus Christ himself. Mrs Lawrence was an intelligent and, in some ways, sophisticated woman, but the conviction she expressed would soon come to be regarded as primitive and naïve, even by many Christians. How its growing rarity has affected the experience of old age would be very hard to calculate, but it must have made a major difference.

Since most funerals still take place in church, many of the attendants are likely to hear assurances about meetings in the afterlife that they no longer believe. One of the early set-pieces in Joyce's *Ulysses* is a description of the funeral of Paddy Dignam seen through the eyes of Leopold Bloom, a Jew who has converted to Catholicism but is still very much an outsider. Noting what a fat belly the priest has (like a bloated sheep), his eye is caught by another cleric who is shaking holy water over the four corners of Dignam's coffin. The thought that this has to be done over every coffin that comes into the chapel makes him wonder what harm there would be if the cleric could see who it was he was shaking his 'stick with a knob at the end' over, and leads to one of those lists Joyce is so fond of (although in this case it is uncharacteristically as well as mercifully short): 'Every mortal day a fresh batch: middle-aged men, old women, children, women dead in childbirth, men with beards, bald-headed business men, consumptive girls with pigeon breasts.' This sense of the sheer multiplicity of corpses will lead Bloom a little later to worry about overcrowding (couldn't they be all buried standing up?) and to entertain those macabre fancies about putrescence which so outdo Claudio in *Measure for Measure*. Given the supposed fertility of graveyards might there not be a trade in human manure: 'Every man his price. Well preserved fat corpse gentleman, epicure, invaluable for fruit garden. A bargain'? It is as Bloom is emerging from the chapel, after a fellow mourner has reminded him of the English version Protestants use of the words they have presumably just heard in Latin, that the question of the afterlife is raised. '*I am the resurrection and the life*. That touches a man's inmost heart', says his companion but, while agreeing, Bloom has his own silent thoughts:

> Your heart perhaps but what price the fellow in the six by two with his toes to the daisies? No touching that. Seat of the affections. Broken heart. A pump after all, pumping thousands of gallons of blood every day. One fine day it gets bunged up

and there you are. Lots of them lying around here: lungs, hearts, livers. Old rusty pumps: damn the thing else. The resurrection and the life. Once you are dead you are dead. That last day idea. Knocking them all up out of their graves. Come forth, Lazarus! And he came fifth and lost the job. Get up! Last day! Then every fellow mousing around for his liver and his lights and the rest of his traps.[6]

It is not hard to see from this short passage why it took so long for *Ulysses* to be published in Catholic Ireland yet it has some of that colloquial verve, and astonishing command of different linguistic registers, which have helped to make the novel widely and rightly recognised as one of the comic masterpieces of European literature. To Mrs Lawrence, however, it would hardly have given much comfort.

Without the promise of an afterlife funerals become more difficult, yet partly also this is because it is so hard to actually mourn *for* the dead rather than feel sorry for one's own loss. 'She dwelt among the untrodden ways / Beside the springs of Dove', writes Wordsworth in one of the best short poems in English, and he goes on to describe how his mysterious subject is now in her grave. Yet his final thought is not so much for the dead girl as 'oh, / The difference to me!' Keats famously referred to Wordsworth's work as belonging to the 'egotistically sublime' and, in a poem in which he praised Wordsworth's originality, Shelley nevertheless complained that he had 'as much imagination / As a pint pot; – he never could / Fancy another situation, / From which to dart his contemplation, / Than that wherein he stood.' Yet in this particular instance, Wordsworth's lament about the difference the death of 'Lucy' has meant for him personally only illustrates the difficulty we all have in not thinking of the death of another in terms of our own selfish concerns. As proof of this, Wordsworth could have quoted the first verse of a poem on the death of Dr Robert Levet, a close friend, by Dr Johnson, someone who is not regarded as particularly egotistical:

Condemn'd to hope's delusive mine,
As on we toil from day to day,
By sudden blasts, or slow decline,
Our social comforts drop away.

---

6. From *Peter Bell the Third*.

Johnson was undoubtedly sad that Robert Levet was no more but his main thought is, like Wordsworth's, not in fact for the dead but for those still living. In a life which he describes in that striking but all too typical opening metaphor (are all our hopes delusive?), he is thinking not so much of what it means to Levet to be dead, a perhaps impossible line of enquiry, but how his own existence is impoverished by the absence of yet one more social resource.

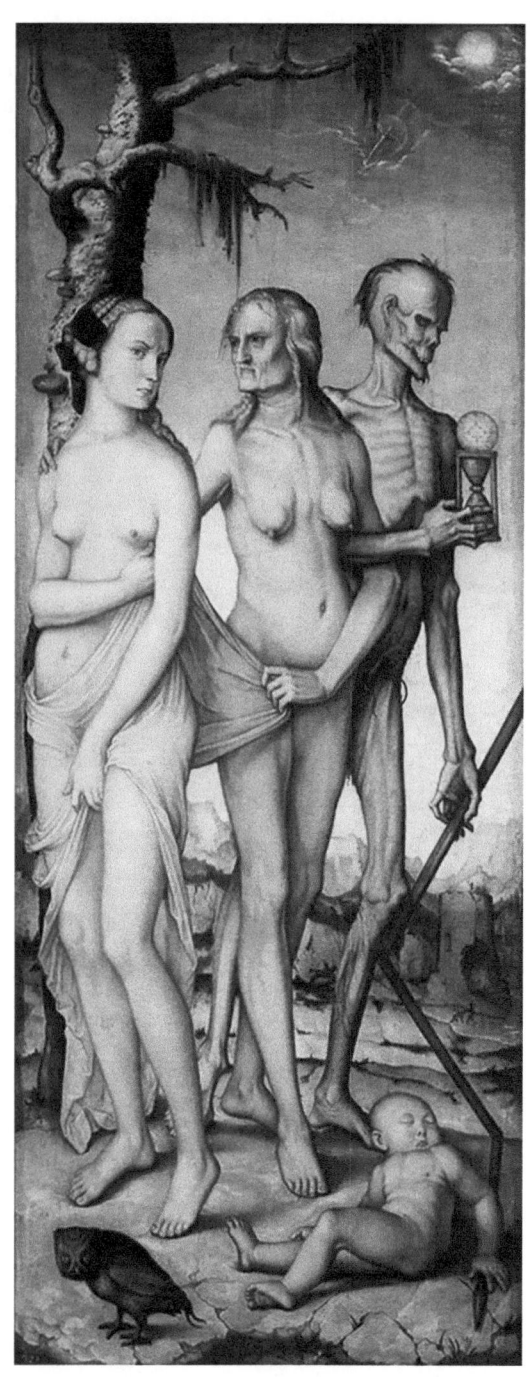

The Ages of Woman and Death
Painting by Hans Baldung, 1541-44. Prado Museum, Madrid

12

Postscript: On 'the Stages of Life'

When people look back on their lives, either nostalgically or with a view to taking stock, they sometimes find it convenient to divide the past into periods or phases. These are what used to be known as the ages of man, the application to women being far less common for reasons too familiar to mention. I have already recalled that for Jaques, in *As You Like It*, there were seven of these and his famous speech is among the best known in Shakespeare, one of those few that, in the days when learning verse was fashionable, used to be recited as a party piece by aspiring young thespians. Which speeches in Shakespeare become so well-known that they are embedded in the national consciousness is a stranger business than it might at first appear. The most familiar of them to the British population as a whole is surely Hamlet's 'To be or not to be?', although anyone who takes the trouble to move on beyond these opening words soon realises how gloomy a vision of everyday life it offers, so much so that its upshot seems to be that there would be no point in living on were it not for anxieties about what is likely to happen once we were dead.

Jaques' description of the seven ages of man may not be quite so well-known but is equally pessimistic, so one might be led to wonder whether there is something morbid in the national psyche that favours doom and gloom. It is a strange choice in any case given that it is hardly an integral part of *As You Like It* but seems to have been largely intended by Shakespeare as a filler. The young Orlando has burst in on the exiled Duke Senior and his companions with his sword drawn and demanded food for Adam, whom he has left in another part of the Forest of Arden after the old man fainted from hunger. Pacified by the welcome he receives, he exits briefly so that he can fetch Adam and it is in the short interval before he returns that the Duke and his courtiers are obliged to 'talk among themselves' and Jaques fills the space with his ages of man speech.

It takes someone with a dark view of human existence not to find anything pleasant in early childhood but for Jaques it is largely a matter, in those powerful words that have been instrumental in making what he says so familiar, of 'mewling and puking'. Schooldays often evoke happy memories but for him they are chiefly represented by the whining young scholar who drags himself to school at a snail's pace. If Shakespeare himself had been so unwilling to pursue his education at that early stage, he would have been one of the most striking examples of late development in human history. The various other stages are not equally spaced out so that youth is divided between a very briefly sketched lover, 'sighing like a furnace', and a soldier whose heroism is devalued by his search for what is, after all, only a '*bubble* reputation'. The choice of soldiering as a vocation for a young man is somewhat arbitrary but much more so is how Jaques chooses to represent what many would consider as the most important 'age', and what is almost always the longest. The form of this speech does, of course, make arbitrariness unavoidable but it seems slightly strange that this middle stretch of time is wholly occupied by the 'justice', with a stomach as well lined with food as his clothing is likely to be with fur, not so much Falstaff's friend Robert Shallow but a magistrate in all the pomp of prosperous middle age. Dealing with all the different possible occupations of middle life in this exclusive and necessarily summary way means that Jaques still has room for two final categories, but there is enough physical detail in his description of the 'pantaloon', with his slippers, spectacles, thin legs, man-bag and shrill reedy voice, to make the seventh and final stage seem redundant. In any case, '*sans* everything' hardly qualifies as a real phase of living at all.

The pessimism of Jaques' vision of the whole course of human life is intensified by the way he sees it in a theatrical context, with men and women walking on stage to play their parts and then walking off, as if the whole thing were no more than an afternoon or evening performance. But then as the commentators have often been keen to point out, Jaques corresponds to many far from flattering Elizabethan stereotypes of not only the melancholic but also the traveller, the kind of person who, as Rosalind puts it at one point, has sold his own lands in order to see those of others. These critics have been happy to accept the hostile analysis of his attitude offered in the seventh scene of Act 2 by Duke Senior, who has retreated to form a would-be idyllic community in the

Forest of Arden after having been forcibly removed from power by his younger brother. He relates Jacques' jaundiced view of human life back to defects in his own character and implicitly defines him as a cynic. Yet, if he is indeed a cynic, the opinions Jaques expresses on the cruelty of hunting probably strike even more of a chord now than they did at the time, and the fact that he is so appreciative of the clown or jester, Touchstone, chimes with a common feeling that human relations present such a depressing catalogue of misery and distress that humour is the only appropriate response (a view I have been tempted to attribute to Beckett, conscious though I am of how fiercely he resented any attempt to pigeonhole him).

Whether or not Jaques' seven ages of man speech is accurately described as cynical may be a moot point but one of its obvious features is an emphasis that is uniquely masculine. In a period when it was almost impossible for women to become soldiers or magistrates, this is hardly surprising, although in the work of the Renaissance painter Hans Baldung, there does seem to have been an unusual predilection for depicting the stages in *female* lives. One of his paintings is known as *The Ages of Woman and Death* and shows a baby in the foreground and then two naked women, one young and the other distinctly old, in facial features and breasts at least, who are very close to each other. Linking arms with the older woman is a skeletal angel of death, a memento mori carrying the traditional hourglass and no doubt reminding some viewers that Baldung had been a pupil of Albrecht Dürer. Quite how to read all the symbols in the painting is not easy, especially after we learn that it is part of a diptych, the second panel of which is a cheerful representation of *The Three Graces*. According to Lynn Botelho, the younger woman in the first painting shows signs of being pregnant, while the way the old woman's body is represented, in its bottom half at least, could be construed as 'an invitation to the sexual act' which the totality of her body predicts will be vain. That is to say that the painting as a whole conveys, in her view, a Northern European feeling that sex is only permissible if its aim is reproduction, as well as 'the profound fear' raised in the period by 'the sexuality of old women'. This would mean that Baldung is dealing with themes similar to those the Restoration dramatists I previously mentioned took up (although in a much lighter vein!), or Pope is evoking when he imagines his former society beauties as witches.

Envisaging life as having seven rather than three divisions allows more room for reflecting on what is characteristic of each but that task is difficult and, if the notion of what is appropriately 'age-related' has always been a challenge, it appears to become more so every day. I have already mentioned the paradox of the Americans having a president who is in his seventies while, as I write, France is in turmoil over attempts by theirs to adjust the retirement age for men and women in a way that reflects their increased longevity. Because no one likes to give up an advantage, these are conflicts here that have taken or are likely to take place all over Europe, as well as in other countries beyond, challenges which hardly suggest that affixing set characteristics to each stage of life is becoming easier with time – but then neither does watching a Swedish girl solemnly addressing the United Nations on climate change while she is still in her teens (and looking even younger).

Greta Thunberg is an illustration that 'the ages of man' have never been set in stone and that the characteristics attributed to each can be transferable. In *The Ages of Man: A Study in Medieval Writing and Thought*, a scholarly investigation into just how many of them it was customary to envisage in medieval literature, J.A. Burrow has provided illustrations of how the supposed attributes of one stage are not limited to it alone. The most familiar example he gives is of the so-called *puer senex* (a good deal of medieval literature is in Latin), someone who, just like Greta Thunberg, is an adolescent or child yet with all the apparent wisdom of the old. The prototype here is the young Jesus holding his own with the theological scholars in the Temple, but another reasonably precocious young person is invoked by first Shylock and then Gratiano when, in *The Merchant of Venice*, the youthful Portia is disguised as a lawyer and hailed as a 'Daniel come to judgement'. This reference is to that part of the Apocrypha in which we find Daniel, who is first described as a young boy, exposing the falsehoods of two elders and, thereby, saving Susanna from execution.

In *Love's Labour's Lost*, the absurd Spanish grandee, Don Armado, has a tiny page (his 'tender juvenal') called Moth who astonishes everyone with a wit and understanding far beyond his years. It would have been a part originally easy to cast because Shakespeare's company always included a number of young boy actors who were chiefly trained to play female parts; and this was also a time when there was competition from companies entirely made up of boys playing adult roles. Part of the appeal must have been a fascination with the aspect of the *puer senex* Moth illustrates, and it reappeared in the nineteenth century with the popularity of precocious child actors. The great Shakespearean Edmund Kean began his career as one of those but was soon overtaken by a boy called William Betty who had an enormous following and was known as the young Rocius after a legendary Roman actor from classical times.

The reason Kean could not compete was that he grew up. Dickens has wonderful fun with the vogue for these children with adult capabilities in *Nicholas Nickleby*, in which the hero falls in with a theatrical troupe led by a Mr Vincent Crummles. One of the stars of this troupe is Crummles' daughter who is eighteen but seems twelve, having been kept looking young by a diet of gin, and who is known as 'the infant phenomenon'.

Examples such as these are not hard to find and are in any event a digression that I can blame on the lure of youth. Much rarer are instances in which old people are able to take on the qualities of the young, *senex puer* as it were: it seems easier, that is, for human beings to anticipate adult qualities than shed or replace the ones they have already acquired. Those British music-hall stars of former times, such as Wee Georgie Wood or Jimmie Clitheroe, who were able to impersonate little boys well into their fifties, are hardly good counter-examples in that what they were doing in their art was compensating for the misfortune of physical underdevelopment. 'Unless you be converted to become as little children', says the New Testament, 'you shall not enter into the kingdom of heaven' (Matthew 18:3). What these famous words are often taken to mean is that old people have somehow to rediscover the innocence of youth, and that kind of ingenuous faith which children often have; that they need to forget all those experiences of the world and human nature (that have presumably been instrumental in making Jaques something of a cynic) and wipe the slate clean. But that is a kind of innocence which the cynical would put down to lack of experience, and a kind of trust they would largely ascribe to ignorance. Whether that is a correct interpretation or not, it is clearly easier to learn new habits than abandon old ones so that the childlike qualities which the old might be expected to adopt in this transference of attributes are likely to turn out to be of the wrong kind. Second childhood is not a qualification for the kingdom of heaven in characters such as Proust's Baron Charlus, and very many others, but rather the hell of senile dementia.

Not everybody has seen dementia as a hell. At the end of the medieval period a book by Erasmus appeared that was a success all over Europe and called *In Praise of Folly*. It is Folly herself who addresses the reader and refers to 'burdensome old age, not only hateful to others, but to itself also'. Yet she congratulates herself on being able to bring the old to 'the spring of our handmaid Lethe' where they may 'drink large drafts of oblivion and thus by gradually dissipating their cares grow young once again'. Some would say that the old thereby lose their grip on reality and develop wandering minds but isn't that, Folly asks, essentially what it means to be a child and do not old people become in this process more pleasant as drinking companions, especially in comparison with those who have to bear all the 'wretched worries of mature life'. Childlike themselves, is it any wonder the old get on so well with children: '"Like will to like", quoth the devil to the collier.' For, after all, what difference is there between an old man and a child except that one has more wrinkles? Do not they both have 'whitish hair, toothless gums' and weakness of body; do not both 'stutter and babble and engage in tomfoolery'; are not both 'forgetful and thoughtless'? What I do, Folly boasts, in giving a man a second childhood, is restore him to 'the happiest part of his life', and she goes on, 'if men would refrain completely from any contact with wisdom and live their entire lives with me, they would not be any old age at all. Instead they would enjoy perpetual youth and live happily ever after.' All of which might be comforting, if only one were able to discount the irony.

It is not only any potential transference of qualities between the generations, either upwards or downwards, which makes it difficult to apply Jaques' seven ages of man to the modern world, but also that startling extension of the lifespan about which Camilla Cavendish was so concerned. Perhaps, however, they were never a close fit, especially as the main, initial reason for lighting on the number seven seems to have been because it corresponded with the seven planets. In his detailed account of the alternatives on offer in the Middle Ages, Burrow describes one that was based on four divisions, corresponding to the four seasons (whereas in the planetary scenario Saturn was ascribed to old age, there are no prizes for guessing which of the seasons it was linked with in this). A third option, favoured by Aristotle and Dante, consisted of only three divisions, namely growth, stasis and decline. Its simplicity makes it attractive; yet one of the epigraphs to Burrow's book is an extract from a work by Petrarch expressing scepticism about the usefulness of any divisions at all. Like Erasmus' book, the original is in Latin, which Burrow translates as:

> Some divide our narrow little life into four parts, some into six, some into even more. In this way they seek to extend that smallest of things by increasing, not the length, which cannot be, but the number of the parts. But what is the use of such divisions? Invent as many little parts as you please, they vanish every one almost at once, in the twinkling of an eye.

In their *Rethinking Old Age: Theorising the Fourth Age*, Paul Higgs and Chris Gilleard refer to what is today widely recognised as the 'third age': that time of life in which retired people take exercise classes to keep themselves limber, improve their minds by learning new languages and either polish up old skills or acquire quite new ones. These are practices associated with a term whose success can perhaps be judged by the fact that it is has a university named after it, England being by no means the only country to have a 'university of the third age'. Yet the effect of this success, according to these two writers, is to help 'push to the margins those aspects of later life that are most discomforting, distressing and, indeed, disgusting'. The result is that a 'fourth age emerges as a re-imagined old age where all the undesirable elements of later life cluster together to create a symbolic order on the margins of everyday life'.

The notion of a 'symbolic order' is usually associated with the psychoanalytic theory of Jacques Lacan and was characterised by Terry Eagleton, in the introduction to the 2006 reissue of his *Criticism and Ideology*, in this way:

> The work of Jacques Lacan recasts [the] Hegelian opposition between knowledge and truth as one between the ego and the Other, or the Imaginary and the Symbolic, the former being understood as our inert, largely illusory presence to ourselves and to the objects of our desire, while *the latter signifies that realm of Otherness which, as a site of the truth of the human subject, sets such consciousness in place but forever eludes its puny grasp.* [my italics]

Yet quite what purpose the term is serving here is not clear to me although, taking the word symbolic in its more usual sense, possible representatives of this fourth age could well be Beckett's Nell and Nagg in what Helen Small accurately describes as their 'reduced lives'. In *The Long Life*, she reads *Endgame* through the prism of Theodor Adorno's thoughts on the play and quotes him at one point claiming that the level at which its two old people live is one where, 'Everything waits to be carried off to the dump. This stratum is not a symbolic one but rather the stratum characteristic of a post-psychological condition such as one finds in old people and in those who have been tortured.' This is not a cheerful prospect and neither is Adorno's description of *Endgame* as 'the true gerontology. According to the measure of socially useful labour, which they can no longer perform, old people are superfluous and must be discarded'; Beckett's play 'trains the viewer', he claims, 'for a condition where everyone expects – upon lifting the lid from the nearest dumpster – to find his own parents'.

Yet, if Nell and Nagg can indeed be taken to represent the fourth age, it may be of some comfort that, for Higgs and Gilleard, the concept is 'primarily a social imaginary ... a product less of nature than of the "social mind"'. There seems to me an implication here that to consider the way we think about the last stages of life as anything other than 'a social imaginary' might be to open oneself to that charge of 'ageism' which appears to haunt several of the more literary commentators on the topic whom I mention in my introduction. I said there that no one could deny that 'old age' is to some extent a social construct. Near the beginning of an excellent book entitled *The Midlife Mind: Literature and the Art of Ageing*, which appeared in 2020, Ben Hutchinson writes that 'how we "age" – how we see ourselves *as* ageing – has always been determined by the norms and models surrounding us. We are only as old as others make us feel', and he goes on a little later to refer to a 'constantly shifting process of triangulation between my own self-image and that of society around me'. True as this is, it seems to me also that entering into this negotiation between self and society are factors such as 'bone fractures, cancer, heart disease, arthritis, infections', as well as, on the cognitive side, 'loss of memory, deterioration of problem-solving ability', not to mention Alzheimer's and mild or severe forms of senile dementia. This list of factors is not mine but that of Mary Mothersill when she gave her presidential address on 'Old Age' to the American Philosophical Association in 1999. In an important contribution to a collection of essays published in 2020 on *Literature and Ageing*, nearly all of which dealt with contemporary texts, Helen Small returned to what Mothersill had said and described how she had voiced suspicion of a tendency in 'old-style gerontology' to gloat over the misfortunes she itemised. Small describes how Mothersill first thanked 'the positive gerontologists for shifting the tone', before then adding 'but the unwelcome "facts" remain'. It does not strike me as ageism to agree that indeed they do.

Whether or not there is an ideology of ageism that can be detected in many of the writers I quote, or in my choosing them, a majority certainly share that gloomy view of life which I identify in Jaques, although one practical consideration perhaps to bear in mind is that, in that past which most of the writers inhabit, the material conditions of living on into old age were much more challenging than they are now. Moreover, although Nina Taunton declares that an ambiguity of attitude is the theme of her enquiry into the depiction of old age in early modern England, with disgust at decay on the one hand and praise for the acquisition of wisdom on the other, there seems to me far more interesting material available on the first side of the equation than the second,

Cicero notwithstanding. Coming nearer to our own time, there is, it is true, a long poem by Longfellow called 'Morituri Salutamus', which in the vernacular means 'a salute from those about to die' and which was written for the 50th anniversary of his own 'Class of 1825' of Bowdoin College, the prestigious liberal arts university in New England he had attended (along with Nathaniel Hawthorne). Towards the end of it, Longfellow makes additions to Cicero's list of men who have achieved great things in old age. 'Ah, nothing is too late', he writes:

> *Till the tired heart shall cease to palpitate.*
> *Cato learned Greek at eighty; Sophocles*
> *Wrote his grand Oedipus, and Simonides*
> *Bore off the prize of verse from his compeers,*
> *When each had numbered more than fourscore years.*

He goes on to give other instances of creativity in old age, additional to the ones he cites here, and concludes with an effective final image: 'And as the evening twilight fades away / The sky is filled with stars, invisible by day.'

Longfellow's cheering words are quoted in the chapter entitled 'Literature By and On the Aged' in *Senescence: The Last Half of Life* by the nineteenth-century American psychologist, G. Stanley Hall. He is almost only now remembered as the man who in 1909, as the first president of Clark University, invited Freud to give a number of lectures in America; but this is unfair and his book is full of sensible remarks. Towards the end of it, after admitting that many of the old are like 'battered, water-logged, leaky derelicts … afloat only because they have struck no fatal rocks or because the storms have not quite yet swamped them', he sees a role for the remainder as guides into the future since they have 'the aloofness, impartiality, and power of generalisation that age can best supply'. We need those with 'the sapience long life alone can give', he claims, 'prophets with vision who can inspire and also castigate, to convict the world of sin, righteousness and judgement'. The function of the old is 'to finish a structure that still lacks an upper story and give it an outlook or conning tower from which man can see more clearly the far horizon and take his bearings now and then by the eternal stars', those same stars, perhaps, to which Longfellow referred.

Hall is praising that wisdom of the elders which Eliot scorns and I am aware that, if the optimistic note he strikes has not often been heard up to this point, the reason may not only be a relative dearth of material, or the degree of chance or accident inevitably involved in choosing texts, but also the operation of a certain degree of temperamental affinity. Dr Johnson, for example, is one of the writers on whom I have often relied and who is not noted for his optimism; yet, as I must have already made clear, I am strongly drawn not only to what he says but also to the way he writes. In that life of his friend, Richard Savage, mentioned above, there is a fine passage that describes the expedients Savage employed to hide from himself the meagre success of his literary career. Always ready to defer to 'the suffrages of mankind when they were given in his favour', Johnson writes, his friend 'contented himself with the applause of men of judgement, and was somewhat disposed to exclude all those from the character of men of judgement who did not applaud him'. When one of his works had a poor sale, he attributed the failure to its having appeared during a period 'when the town was empty', the public engrossed with some major issue, or to the refusal of its publishers to promote it adequately, laying the blame 'rather on any other person than the author'. In a surprising turn, Johnson next suggests that, 'although it were doubtless to be wished that truth and reason were universally prevalent', these methods Savage employed to 'live at peace with himself' might be adopted by us all, given how little tranquillity and happiness there is in the world. However, he soon dispenses with this 'pleasing intoxication' and moves into a magisterial and general summing up of Savage's character:

> By imputing none of his miseries to himself, he continued to act upon the same principles, and to follow the same path; was never made wiser by his sufferings, nor preserved by one misfortune from falling into another. He proceeded throughout his life to tread the same steps on the same circle; always applauding his past conduct, or at least forgetting it, to amuse himself with phantoms of happiness which were dancing before him; and willingly turned his eyes from the light of reason, when it would have discovered the illusion, and shown him, what he never wished to see, his real self.

In John Donne's 'Satire III', truth is imagined as being on a huge hill, 'cragged and steep', so that 'he that will / Reach her, about must and about must go, / And what the hill's suddenness resists, win so.' Johnson is employing in prose similar, although more elaborate, rhythmic effects to suggests the difficulty of arriving at an accurate estimate of one's place in the world. There are, of course, many contexts in which it would be naïve to think we could ever reach what Donne refers to as the truth, and Freud is not the only person to have suggested we can never ourselves know our 'real state'. Yet what the rhythm of Johnson's prose suggests is that, in spite of the remarks of Clive James on autobiography, or those of Helene Deutsch on reminiscence, it is the effort that counts.

It is a paradox that some of us can enjoy reading passages like the one above when what it has to say is so depressing. In his attempt to come to terms with not old but middle age, Ben Hutchinson adopted an approach a little like mine in describing how one might deal with its problems. 'By outsourcing our anxiety to minds greater than our own', he wrote, 'we can use literature and culture to help us channel our thoughts and feelings. Through bibliotherapy, we can learn to accept growing older.' But does it help people to accept growing not older but *old* when the majority of the witnesses called are as pessimistic as most of mine have been? The question is allied to the old conundrum about how we can sit through a performance of *King Lear* and say we enjoyed it (though Johnson couldn't). Jenefer Robinson is a philosopher who tries to come to terms with this famous dilemma in her *Deeper than Reason: Emotion and Its Role in Literature, Music and Art.* Discussing Shakespeare's Sonnet 73, the one that begins, 'That time of year thou mayst in me behold', she correctly identifies its subject matter as 'the inevitability of old age and death', but then suggests, in a detailed analysis owing much to the American literary critic Wayne Booth, that the artful way in which the poem is put together engages its reader in psychological processes that provide a 'coping mechanism' for dealing with its content. This is analogous to the way 'tragedies both present painful material and at the same time provide the resources for us to cope with this material' and part of their method for doing so, according to Robinson, consists in providing a countervailing pleasure in artistic form.

I admit to being unable to estimate how far this is true in the cases of the passages I cite, given that the satisfaction I take in certain texts of a gloomy nature may well be what Freud taught us to call 'overdetermined'. Certainly, one element I find appealing in several of them is a species of dark humour, which is perhaps an even better example of a 'coping mechanism' than Robinson's artistic form. It is this that several of those supposed last words quoted in my last chapter would seem to illustrate and that, when they are uttered *in extremis*, are known as gallows humour. In Joyce's representation of what are mainly Bloom's thoughts at Paddy Dignam's funeral, the humour is rather that of the graveyard. As the cemetery's caretaker is leading the funeral party to the spot where Dignam will be buried, he describes how on one misty evening two drunks had come looking for the grave of an old friend of theirs called

Mulcahy that had recently been adorned by his widow with a statuette of Jesus. When they finally found the grave, one of them was sober enough to be able to spell out their friend's name while the other, 'blinking up at the sacred figure', blurted out *'Not a bloody bit like the man ... That's not Mulcahy, ... whoever done it.'* 'You must laugh sometimes so better do it that way', Bloom reflects a little later, and then adds, 'Gravediggers in *Hamlet*.' The first gravedigger in that play is certainly a comedian but the mood becomes more sombre when Hamlet, holding the skull of a court jester he knew well ('poor Yorick'), asks, 'Where be your gibes now, your gambols, your songs, your flashes of merriment that were wont to set the table on a roar?' as if to indicate the limits humour has in allowing us to cope.

When Petrarch notes that, however many stages life is divided into, it has at some point to come to an end, his remarks recall Zeno's reflections on the flightpath of an arrow. As the philosopher George puts it, in *Jumpers*, Tom Stoppard's witty 1972 play, 'since an arrow shot towards a target first had to cover half the distance, and then half the remainder, and then half the remainder after that, and so on *ad infinitum*', Zeno's famous paradox was that 'it never quite gets there'. Here is help for the aged, one might think, giving the lie to all those iconic, eroticised images of Saint Sebastian, tied to a tree and with arrows sticking out of him, except that George then takes care to add that, if the martyred saint in question may not have been *shot* dead, he nevertheless 'died of fright'.

List of Works Cited

In the case of Shakespeare, Jane Austen, Balzac, and Dickens reference to specific editions here would be pointless because so many are available. All I have tried to do, as far as these writers are concerned, is list the relevant works in chronological order although, as far as Shakespeare is concerned, that is a notoriously speculative affair.

Translations from the French are mostly my own. Aging versus ageing is a transatlantic dispute I have not attempted to solve.

Adorno, Theodor W., 'Trying to understand *Endgame*', trans. Michael T. Jones, *New German Critique*, no. 26 (Spring/Summer 1982), pp. 119-50
Allen, Woody, *Without Feathers* (New York: Ballantine Books, 1983)
Améry, Jean, *On Aging: Revolt and Resignation*, trans. John D. Barlow (Bloomington: Indiana University Press, 1994) (The original German edition came out in 1968.)
Amis, Kingsley, *Lucky Jim* (1954); *The Old Devils* (1986)
Arendt, Hannah, 'The Concept of History: Ancient and Modern', in idem, *Between Past and Future: Six Exercises in Political Thought* (New York: Viking, 1961), pp. 41-90
Arnold, Matthew, *On Translating Homer* (Charleston: Nabu Press, 2012 [1861])
Athill, Diane, *Somewhere Towards the End* (London: Granta Books, 2008)
———, *Stet* (London: Granta Books, 2010)
Austen, Jane, *Sense and Sensibility* (1811)
———, *Pride and Prejudice* (1813)
———, *Emma* (1816)
———, *Persuasion* (1818)
Balzac, Honoré, *La Peau de chagrin* (1831); *Le Père Goriot* (1835); *La Cousine Bette* (1846)
Beauvoir, Simone de, *Une Mort très douce* (Paris: Gallimard, 1964)
———, *La Vieillesse* (Paris: Gallimard, 1970)
Beckett, Samuel, *The Complete Dramatic Works* (London: Faber & Faber, 1986)
Beerbohm, Max, *Enoch Soames: A Memory of the 1890s* (Madrid: HardPress Publishing, 2010)
Boswell, James, *The Life of Samuel Johnson* (London: Penguin, 2008 [1791])

Botelho, Lynn, 'Les Trois Âges et la Mort du peintre Hans Baldung (XVIe siècle)', *Clio*, Vol. 42 (2015)

Boym, Svetlana, *The Future of Nostalgia* (New York: Basic Books, 2001)

Browning, Robert, *The Poetical Works of Robert Browning: Complete from 1833 to 1868 and the Shorter Poems Thereafter* (Oxford: Oxford University Press, 1953)

Bufford, S., *A Discourse Against Unequal Marriages* (1696)

Burgess, Anthony, *Shakespeare* (London: Jonathan Cape, 1970)

Burrow, J.A., *The Ages of Man: A Study in Medieval Writing and Thought* (Oxford: Clarendon Press, 1988)

Carroll, Lewis, *Selected Poems* (London: Penguin, 2012)

Cavendish, Camilla, *Extra Time: Ten Lessons for an Ageing World* (London: HarperCollins, 2019)

Charney, Maurice, *Wrinkled Deep in Time: Aging in Shakespeare* (New York: Columbia University Press, 2009)

Chase, Karen, *The Victorians and Old Age* (Oxford: Oxford University Press, 2009)

Chaucer, Geoffrey, *The Canterbury Tales*, ed. Jill Mann (London: Penguin, 2005)

Chekhov, Anton, *The Steppe and Other Stories, 1887-1891*, trans. Ronald Wilks (London: Penguin, 2001)

———, *Plays of Anton Chekhov* (London: Penguin, 2002)

Cicero, Marcus Tullius, *Treatises on Friendship and Old Age*, trans. Evelyn S. Shuckburgh (Pantianos Classics) (First published in 1910.)

Congreve, William, *The Way of the World* (London: New Mermaids, 2002)

Cummings, Bruce Frederick ('W.N.P. Barbellion'), *The Journal of a Disappointed Man* (London: Hogarth Press, 1984 [1919])

Dickens, Charles, *Nicholas Nickleby* (1839); *The Old Curiosity Shop* (1841); *Martin Chuzzlewit* (1844); *Little Dorrit* (1857); *Great Expectations* (1861); *Our Mutual Friend* (1865)

Donne, John, *John Donne's Poetry*, ed. Donald R. Dickson (New York: W.W. Norton & Co., 2007)

Duncan-Jones, Katherine, *Shakespeare: An Ungentle Life* (London: Methuen Drama, 2010)

Eagleton, Terry, *Criticism and Ideology: A Study in Marxist Literary Theory* (London: Verso, 2006)

Edgeworth, Maria, *Castle Rackrent*, ed. George Watson (Oxford: Oxford University Press, 1984)

Eliot, George, *Middlemarch: A Study of Provincial Life* (1871-72)

Eliot, T.S., *The Poems of T.S. Eliot*, ed. Christopher Ricks and Jim McCue, 2 vols (London: Faber & Faber, 2015)

———, *Selected Essays* (London: Faber & Faber, 1932)

Ellman, Richard, 'Yeats' Second Puberty', *New York Review of Books*, 9 May 1985

———, *Yeats: The Man and the Masks* (London: Penguin, 1988)

Enfield, Edward, *Old Age and How to Survive It* (Chichester: Summersdale, 2009)
Enright, D.J., *The Faber Book of Fevers and Frets* (London: Faber & Faber, 1989)
——, *Old Men and Comets* (Oxford: Oxford University Press, 1993)
——, *Injury Time: A Memoir* (London: Pimlico, 2003)
Erasmus, *Praise of Folly*, trans. Betty Radice (London: Penguin, 1971)
Freud, Sigmund, *The Pelican Freud Library, Vol. 5: The Psychopathology of Everyday Life*, trans. James Strachey (London: Penguin, 1960)
——, *The Pelican Freud Library, Vol. 6: Jokes and Their Relation to the Unconscious*, trans. James Strachey and Angela Richards (London: Penguin, 1960)
Gibbon, Edward, *Memoirs of My Life and Writings*, ed. A.O.J. Cockshut and Stephen Constantine (Keele: Ryburn Publishing, 1994) (The *Memoirs* were first published in 1796.)
Gray, Simon, *Coda* (London: Faber & Faber, 2008)
Gray, Thomas, *The Poems of Thomas Gray* (Forgotten Books, 2012)
Hall, G. Stanley, *Senescence: The Last Half of Life* (New York: D. Appleton and Company, 1922)
Hamilton, David, *The Monkey Gland Affair* (London: Chatto & Windus, 1900)
Hamilton, Ian, *Keepers of the Flame: Literary Estates and the Rise of Biography* (London: Faber & Faber, 1992)
Harding, D.W., *The Impulse to Dominate* (London: Allen & Unwin, 1941)
Hardy, Thomas, *The Collected Poems of Thomas Hardy* (Ware: Wordsworth, 1994)
Hatherley, Owen, *The Ministry of Nostalgia* (London: Verso Books, 2016)
Hartung, Heike, *Ageing, Gender and Illness in Anglophone Literature: Narrating Age in the Bildungsroman* (New York: Routledge, 2015)
Hayley, William, *A Philosophical, Historical, and Moral Essay on Old Maids*, 3 vols (1785)
Heller, Joseph, *Now and Then: A Memoir from Coney Island to Here* (New York: Scribner, 1999)
Hepworth, Mike, *Stories of Ageing* (Buckingham: Open University Press, 2000)
Higgs, Paul, and Chris Gilleard, *Rethinking Old Age: Theorising the Fourth Age* (London: Palgrave Macmillan, 2015)
Hobbes, Thomas, *Leviathan* (London: Penguin, 2017 [1651])
Hutchinson, Ben, *The Midlife Mind: Literature and the Art of Ageing* (London: Reaktion Books, 2020)
James, Clive, *Unreliable Memoirs* (London: Picador, 2015 [1980])
——, *Latest Readings* (New Haven, CT: Yale University Press, 2015)
——, *Sentenced to Life* (London: Picador, 2015)
——, *Injury Time* (London: Picador, 2017)
James, Henry, *Washington Square* (London: Penguin, 2007)

Jewusiak, Jacob, *Aging, Duration, and the English Novel: Growing Old from Dickens to Woolf* (Cambridge: Cambridge University Press, 2019)
Johnson, Samuel, *The Complete English Poems* (London: Penguin 1982)
——, *Lives of the Poets*, ed. Roger Lonsdale (Oxford: Oxford University Press, 2006)
——, *The Idler, with Additional Essays* (Gale Ecco, 2018)
Jonson, Ben, *Volpone*, ed. Brian Parker and David Bevington (Manchester: Manchester University Press, 1988)
——, *Timber, or Discoveries*, in C.H. Herford, P. Simpson and E. Simpson (eds), *Works of Ben Jonson* (Oxford: Clarendon Press, 1954)
Joseph, Jenny, *Selected Poems* (Hexham: Bloodaxe, 1992)
Joyce, James, *Ulysses* (London: Bodley Head, 1960)
Kinsley, Michael, *Old Age: A Beginner's Guide* (London: Penguin, 2017)
Kurtz, Irma, *About Time: Growing Old Disgracefully* (London: John Murray, 2009)
Lafargue, Paul, *The Right to Be Lazy and Other Writings* (New York: NYRB Classics, 2022)
Larkin, Philip, *Collected Poems*, ed. Anthony Thwaite (London: Faber & Faber, 1988)
Lawrence, D.H., *Women in Love* (London: Penguin, 1995)
——, 'A Propos of Lady Chatterley's Lover', in *Lady Chatterley's Lover* (London: Penguin, 1994)
——, 'The Border-Line', in Selected Short Stories (London: Penguin, 1982)
——, *The Poems*, ed. Christopher Pollnitz, 3 vols (Cambridge University Press, 2013)
Lamb, Charles, *Elia and the Last Essays of Elia*, ed. Jonathan Bate (Oxford: Oxford University Press, 1987)
Locke, John, *Second Treatise of Government and A Letter Concerning Toleration* (Oxford: Oxford University Press, 2016)
Lodge, David, *Deaf Sentence* (London: Penguin, 2009)
Looser, Devoney, *Women Writers and Old Age in Great Britain, 1750-1850* (Baltimore: Johns Hopkins University Press, 2008)
Lucretius, *On the Nature of Things*, trans. Martin Ferguson Smith (Indianapolis: Hackett, 2001)
Macauley, Thomas Babington, *Reviews, Essays and Poems* (London: Ward, Lock & Co., 1890)
MacCarthy, Fiona, *Byron: Life and Legend* (London: John Murray, 2002)
Mankell, Henning, *Quicksand: What It Means to Be a Human Being*, trans. from the Swedish Laurie Thompson with Marlaine Delargy (New York: Vintage Books, 2014)
Martin, Christopher, *Constituting Old Age in Early Modern Literature from Queen Elizabeth to King Lear* (Amherst: University of Massachusetts Press, 2012)
Mauriac, François, *Mémoires intérieurs: Nouveaux mémoires intérieurs* (Paris: Flammarion, 1993)

Montaigne, Michel de, *The Complete Essays*, ed. and trans. M.A. Screech (Harmondsworth, Penguin, 1993)

Mothersill, Mary, 'Old Age', *Proceedings and Addresses of the American Philosophical Association*, Vol. 73, no. 2 (November 1999), pp. 7, 9-23

Orwell, George, 'The Art of Donald McGill', in Sonia Orwell and Ian Angus (eds), *The Collected Essays, Journalism, and Letters of George Orwell* (Harmondsworth: Penguin, 1968), Vol. 2

Port, Cynthia, and Aagje Swinnen, 'Age Studies Comes of Age', *Age, Culture, Humanities: An Interdisciplinary Journal*, Vol. 1 (January 2015), pp. 1-8

Pope, Alexander, *The Major Works* (Oxford: Oxford University Press, 1994)

Prior, Matthew, *The Literary Works of Matthew Prior*, ed. H. Bunker Wright and M.K. Spears, 2 vols (Oxford: Clarendon Press, 1971)

Proust, Marcel, *À la recherche du temps perdu* (Paris: Grasset and Gallimard, 1913-27); available in English as *Remembrance of Things Past*, trans. C.K. Scott Moncrieff and Terence Kilmartin (London: Penguin, 1984-85)

Richards, I.A., *Practical Criticism: A Study of Literary Judgment* (London: Routledge & Kegan Paul, 1971)

Richardson, Catherine, 'Continuity and Memory: Domestic Space, Gesture and Affection at the Sixteenth-Century Deathbed', in Antony Buxton, Linda Hulin and Jane Anderson (eds), *In Habit: People, Places and Possessions* (Oxford: Peter Lang, 2017)

Richardson, Catherine. '"Make you a cloak of it and weare it for my sake": material culture and commemoration in early modern English towns', in Penman, M. (ed.) *Monuments and Monumentality Across Medieval and Early Modern Europe.* (Lincolnshire: Shaun Tyas, 2013)

Robb, Graham, *Balzac* (London: Picador, 1994)

Robinson, Jenefer, *Deeper than Reason: Emotion and Its Role in Literature, Music and Art* (Oxford: Oxford University Press, 2005)

Rousseau, Jean-Jacques, *Discours sur l'origine et les fondements de l'inégalité parmi les hommes* (Paris: Flammarion, 2011)

Routledge, Clay, *Nostalgia: A Psychological Resource* (New York: Routledge, 2016)

Rowe, Nicholas, *The Life of Shakespeare*, with an introduction by Charles Nicholl (London: Pallas Athene, 2009)

Russell, Bertrand, *The Autobiography of Bertrand Russell*, 3 vols (London: G. Allen & Unwin, 1971)

Rutherford, Mark (pen name of William Hale White), *Autobiography* (London: Taylor and Francis, 1976)

Sandy, Mark, '"Strength in What Remains Behind": Wordsworth and the Question of Ageing', *Romanticism*, Vol. 25, no. 3 (2019), pp. 261-70

Shakespeare, William, *Love's Labour's Lost*; *Richard II*; *The Merchant of Venice*; *King Henry IV: Part 1*; *King Henry IV: Part 2*; *King Henry V*; *As You Like It*; *Hamlet*; *Troilus and Cressida*; *Measure for Measure*; *King Lear*; *Macbeth*; *The Tempest*; and the *Sonnets*

Shelley, P.B., *Shelley's Poetry and Prose*, ed. Donald H. Reiman and Neil Fraistat (New York: W.W. Norton & Co., 2002)

Small, Helen, *The Long Life* (Oxford: Oxford University Press, 2007)
——, 'On Not Knowing How to Feel', in Elizabeth Barry and Margery Vibe Skagen (eds), *Literature and Ageing* (London: Boydell & Brewer, 2020)
Southey, Robert, *Poems* (Brookline, MA: Adamant Media Corp., 2001)
Saint-Évremond, Charles de, *Entretiens sur toutes choses*, ed. David Bensoussan (Paris: Desjonquères, 1998)
Stendhal, *La Vie de Henry Brulard* (Paris: Flammarion, 1986)
——, *Journal Littéraire*, in *Œuvres complètes*, Vol. 35, ed. Victor del Litto and Ernest Abravanel (Le Cercle du Bibliophile, 1968)
Sterne, Lawrence, *The Life and Opinions of Tristram Shandy, Gentleman* (London: Penguin, 2009)
Stone, Lawrence, 'Walking over Grandma', *New York Review of Books*, 12 May 1977, pp. 36-38
Stoppard, Tom, *Jumpers* (London: Faber & Faber, 1972)
Swift, Jonathan, *Gulliver's Travels* (Ware: Wordsworth Classics, 1992)
——, *The Complete Poems*, ed. Pat Rogers (London: Penguin, 1983)
Taunton, Nina, *Fictions of Old Age in Early Modern Literature and Culture* (London: Routledge, 2007)
Tennyson, Alfred, Lord, *The Poems of Tennyson*, ed. Christopher Ricks (London: Longmans, 1969)
Thane, Pat, *Old Age in English History: Past Experiences, Present Issues* (Oxford: Oxford University Press, 2000)
Thomas, Dylan, *The Collected Poems of Dylan Thomas* (London: Weidenfeld & Nicolson, 2014)
Thomas, Keith, *Age and Authority in Early Modern England* (London: British Academy, 1976)
Thompson, Denys, *Reading and Discrimination* (London: Chatto & Windus, 1954)
Tolstoy, Leo, *The Death of Ivan Ilyich and Other Stories* (Ware: Wordsworth Classics, 2004)
Tomalin, Claire, *Samuel Pepys: The Unequalled Self* (London: Penguin, 2012)
Trollope, Antony, *The Fixed Period* (CreateSpace, 2017 [1882])
Wada, Shuichi, 'The Status and Understanding of the Elderly in Japan: Understanding the Paternalistic Ideology', in Mike Featherstone and Andrew Wernick (eds), *Images of Aging: Cultural Representations of Later Life* (London: Routledge, 1995)
Wells, H.G., *Tono-Bungay* (London: Penguin, 2005)
Wilde, Oscar, *The Picture of Dorian Gray* (London: Penguin, 2003)
Wiltshire, John, *Frances Burney and the Doctors: Patient Narratives Then and Now* (Cambridge: Cambridge University Press, 2019)
Wolpert, Lewis, *You're Looking Very Well: The Surprising Nature of Growing Old* (London: Faber & Faber, 2011)
Woodward, Kathleen, *Aging and Its Discontents: Freud and Other Fictions* (Bloomington: Indiana University Press, 1991)

—— , 'Telling Stories, Aging, Reminiscence and the Life Review', *Doreen B. Townsend Center Occasional Papers 9* (Berkeley: Doreen B. Townsend Center for the Humanities, UC Berkeley, 1997)

Wordsworth, William, *The Prelude: The Four Texts (1798, 1799, 1805, 1850)* (London: Penguin, 1995)

—— , *Selected Poems* (London: Penguin, 2004)

Yeats, W.B., *Collected Poems of W.B. Yeats* (London: Macmillan & Co. Ltd, 1955)

Zola, Émile, *La Terre* (1887); available in English as *The Earth*, trans. Douglas Parmée (London: Penguin, 2006)

Acknowledgements

I would like to thank my teachers at Downing College, Cambridge, for introducing an ill-educated Northern schoolboy, ignorant as a carp, to so many great works of literature. The novelist Michael Irwin made several useful suggestions about this book, as did Bill Bell, Julian Mannering and John Worthen. Throughout its composition my wife, Geneviève, has provided steady support in the same way that, for more than 50 years now, she has habitually pardoned my French. If a dedication had seemed appropriate, it would have been to her, as well as to 'absent friends'.

Index of Names and Titles

A Propos of Lady Chatterley's Lover 48
Abel, Carl Friedrich 17
Abishag 45
About Time: Growing Old Disgracefully 4, 120
Abraham 55
Addison, Joseph 125, 134
Adorno, Theodor 145
'Age and Authority in Modern England' 22
Ageing, Gender and Illness in Anglophone Literature 5
Ages of Woman and Death, The 141
Aging and its Discontents 30, 97
Aging, Duration and the English Novel 5
Ain't It grand to be blooming well dead 69
Allen, Woody 127
Améry, Jean 28-9, 122
Amis, Kingsley 96, 127, 130
'Animal Tranquillity and Decay' 52, 114
Arendt, Hannah 55
Arnold, Matthew 8
As You Like It 18, 21, 31, 41, 55, 139
Athill, Diana 39, 110, 113, 117
'Aubade' 128
Aurora (Goddess of Dawn) 33
Austen, Jane 9, 57-59, 84, 104

Baldung, Hans 141
Balzac, Honoré de 44-45, 46, 56, 119, 131
Barbauld, Letitia 9
Barbellion, W. N. P. 70, 71,
Beard, Mary 96
'Beautiful Old Age' 18

'Beautiful Young Nymph Going to Bed, A' 40, 42
Beauvoir, Simone de 6-7, 28, 32, 79, 130, 133
Beckett, Samuel 132-133, 145
Beerbohm, Max 68
Being and Nothingness 7
Bennett, Alan 40, 42, 57,
Betty, William 142
'Bishop Orders His Tomb at Saint Praxed's Church, The' 64
Bonnemère, Eugène 79
Booth, Wayne 149
Border-Line, The 129
Boswell, James 33, 127
Botelho, Lynn 141
Boym, Svetlana 89
Braine, John 67
Bridges, Robert 8
Brod, Max 83
Brooke, Rupert 70
Brown, Mrs (Brendan O'Carroll) 42
Browning, Robert 63-64, 134,
Burgess, Anthony 19
Burney, Fanny 9, 114
Burns, Robert 83
Burrow, J. A. 142, 144
Butley 118
Byron, Lord 11, 66, 67, 70, 73, 115, 126

Cameron, David 4
Carroll, Lewis 126-127
Carteret, John 130-131

Castle Rackrent 69
Catch 22 104
Cato (the Elder) 27, 147
Cavendish, Camilla 4, 7, 144
Cézanne, Paul 103
Chambers, Jessie 135
Chaplin, Charlie 27
Charles II 15
Charles V (Holy Roman Empereur) 19
Charney, Maurice 10, 28
Charterhouse of Parma, The 67
Chase, Karen 5, 8
Chaucer, Geoffrey 114, 134
Chekhov, Anton 91, 121-122
Cher 40
Cherry Orchard, The 91
Chevalier, Maurice 11
Cicero 27, 31, 129, 132, 147
Cioffi, Frank 103
Clitheroe, Jimmy 143
Coda 119
Coghill, Neville 77
Coleridge, S. T. 70
Columbus, Christopher 80
Condell, Henry 85
Confessions, Rousseau's 95, 107
Congreve, William 41, 131
Constituting Old Age in Early Modern Literature 5
Cook, Peter 77
Cousine Bette, La 44
Cowley, Abraham 15-16
Criticism and Ideology 145
Critique of Dialectical Reason 7
Cummings, Bruce Frederick 70-72, 104, 116
'Cure' 116
Cyr, Mary 17

Dante 144
Daumier, Honoré 30
David, King 45
Davis, Bette 117
Deaf Sentence 57
Death of Ivan Ilyich, The 120-121
Deeper than Reason 149
Defoe, Daniel 95
Democritus 133
Deutsch, Helene 97, 149

Dickens, Charles 8-9, 22, 78, 79, 80, 81, 143
Dietrich, Marlene 40
Dinnerladies 42
Discourse on Inequality 52
Donne, John 72, 148
Dreary Story, A 122
Duncan-Jones, Katherine 19
Dürer, Albrecht 141
Dylan, Bob 98

Eagleton, Terry 145
Earth (La Terre) 79
'Echo Point' 108
Edgeworth, Maria 69
'Elegy Written in a Country Churchyard' 92
'Elementary Sonnet' 108
Eliot, George 81-82, 113, 114
Eliot, T. S. 2, 36, 52, 96, 106-107, 147
Ellman, Richard 47
Emma 58
Endgame 132, 145
Enfield, Edward 6
Enoch Soames 68
Enright, D. J. 10, 96, 116,117
Epicurus 128
Epistle to a Lady' 131
Erasmus 143
Extra Time: Ten Lessons for an Ageing World 4

Faber Book of Fevers and Frets 116
'Father William' 127
Faure, Félix 103
Fictions of Old Age in Early Modern Literature and Culture 5
Fixed Period, The 80, 81
Four Quartets 36
Freud, Sigmund 30, 43, 89, 97, 147, 149
Future of Nostalgia, The 89

Gainsborough, Thomas 17
Galileo 80
Garbo, Greta 39
George III 126
Gibbon, Edward 16, 18, 95, 104, 106, 108, 113, 116
Gilleard, Chris 144
Gillray, Thomas 59

Index

Goncourt (Brothers) 46
'GP' 117
Gray, Simon 118-119
Gray, Thomas 92, 93
Great Expectations 22
Greer, Germaine 43
Growing Old in America 23
Gulliver's Travels 33
Gurdjieff, George 129

Hall, G. Stanley 49, 147
Hamilton, David 47
Hamilton, Ian 72, 82
Hamlet 32, 150
Happy Days 132
Harding, D. W. 103
Hardy, Thomas 48
Hartung, Heike 5
Hatherley, Owen 89
Hawthorne, Nathaniel 147
Hayley, William 58
Heine, Heinrich 128
Heller, Joseph 104
Heminge, John 85
Henry IV Part One 1
Henry IV Part Two 1, 2, 31, 44, 93
Hepworth, Mike 5
Heraclitus 133
Higgs, Paul 144
Hobbes, Thomas 53, 68, 69, 102, 106
Horace 15, 17
Hutchinson, Ben 146, 149

'I look into my glass' 49
'Ibrutinib' 118
Idler, The 105
Images of Aging 33
'Immortality Ode, The' 92
Impulse to Dominate, The 103
In Praise of Folly 143
Injury Time 10, 118

James, Clive 95-96, 108, 118, 149
James, Henry 59-60
'Japanese Maple' 95-96
Jenkins, Harold 51
Jesus 142, 150
Jewusiak, Jacob 5

Johnson, Samuel 15-16, 33, 105-106, 108, 114, 125-126, 127, 134, 136, 148-149
Jonson, Ben 17, 75-76, 81
Joseph, Jenny 39, 48
Journal of a Disappointed Man, The 70
Joyce, James 61, 68, 135, 149
Jumpers 150
Juvenal 105

Kafka, Franz 82-83
Kean, Edmund 142
Keats, John 71, 136
Keepers of the Flame 72, 83
Kennedy, President John 28
King Lear 4, 17, 19-22, 24-5, 75, 149
Knight, Edward (né Austen) 84
Kurosawa, Akira 32
Kurtz, Irma 4, 101, 120

Lacan, Jacques 145
Lady Chatterley's Lover 47
'Lady's Dressing Room, The' 42
Lafargue, Paul 130
Lamb, Charles 24, 28, 130
Larkin, Philip 48, 93, 127-128
Lawrence, D. H. 18, 35-6, 47-48, 90-91, 92, 96, 116-117, 128-129, 134
Lawrence, Ernest 134
Lawrence, Frieda 48, 129
Lawrence, Mrs Lydia 135, 136
Leavis, F. R. 58
'Leçons des ténèbres' 108
Levet, Robert 136-137
Leviathan 68, 102
Life of Shakespeare (Anthony Burgess) 19
Literature and Aging 146
Little Dorrit 22
Little Gidding 106
Lives of the Poets, The 15, 125
Locke, John 57
Lodge, David 57
Long Life, The 7, 9
Longfellow, Henry Wadsworth 147
Looser, Deveney 5, 9, 58,
Love's Labour's Lost 142
Lucky Jim 96
Lucretius 127
Lyrical Ballads 51-52, 66

Macauley, Catherine 9
Macauley, T. B. 130
Macbeth 17
'"Make your cloak of it and weare it for my sake"' 85
Malade Imaginaire, Le 117
Mankell, Henning 73
Mann, Sir Robert 130
Mansfield, Katherine 128-129
Martin Chuzzlewit 9, 78,
Martin, Christopher 5, 25
Marx, Karl 130
Matthew (New Testament) 143
Mauriac, François 131
McGill, Donald 41
'MCMXIV' 93
Measure for Measure 68, 120, 135
Mémoires intérieurs 131
Memoirs of My Life and Writings (Gibbon) 16
Merchant of Venice, The 21, 142
Michael 55. 63, 75, 92-3
Middlemarch 81-82, 86, 114
Midlife Mind, The 146
Mignon, Elizabeth 41
Milton, John 108, 126
Modest Proposal, A 80
Molière 66, 114, 117
Moll Flanders 95
Montaigne 130, 133
Montesquieu 102
'Morituri Salutamis' 147
Mort Très Douce, Une 7
Mothersill, Mary 146
Murry, John Middleton 129
'My Way' 101

Necker, Jacques 104
Nicholas Nickleby 143
Nixon, Richard 23-4
Nostalgia: A Psychological Resource 89

'Ode on a Distant Prospect of Eton Chapel' 92
Oedipus at Colonus 28
Old Age (La Vieillesse) 6
Old Age and How to Survive It 6
Old Age in English History 3

'Old Cumberland Beggar, The' 51-2,
Old Devils, The 130
'Old Fools, The' 128
'Old Man Travelling' 52
'Old Man's Comforts and How He Gained Them, The' 126
Old Men and Comets 117
Oldie, The 89
On Translating Homer 8
Orwell, George 41, 116
Othello 96
Our Mutual Friend 8
'Ozymandias' 65

Paradise Lost 126
Pardoner's Tale, The 134
Pascal, Blaise 122
Pasquil's Jests 20
Peau de Chagrin, La 120
Pepys, Samuel 114
Persuasion 59
Petrarch 144, 150
Philosophical, Historical, and Moral Essay on Old Maids 58
'Piano' 90-91,
Picture of Dorian Gray, The 40
Piozzi, Hester 9
Plato 27, 114,
Poetzsch, Markus 11
Pope, Alexander 131
Porter, Jane 9
Practical Criticism 90
'Prayer for Old Age, A' 46
Prelude, The 10, 72
Pride and Prejudice 57, 84
Prior, Matthew 114
'Pros and Cons of Reaching Ninety' 122
Proust, Marcel 16, 29-30, 31, 36, 90, 118, 119, 120, 143
Psychopathology of Everyday Life, The 43

Quiney, Thomas 18

Ramesses II 65,
Reading and Discrimination 3
Red and the Black, The 67
Remembrance of Things Past 16, 118
'Resolution and Independence' 114

Index

Rich, Edward 125
Richard II 125
Richards, I. A. 90-91,
Richardson, Catherine 85
Right to Be Lazy, The 130
Riley, Old Mother (Arthur Lucan) 42
Robb, Graham 46
Robinson, Jenefer 149
Room at the Top 67
'Rounded with a Sleep' 108
Rousseau, Jean-Jacques 52-53, 96, 107
Routledge, Clay 89, 98
Rowe, Nicholas 16-17, 19
Rowlandson, Thomas 59
Ruined Cottage, The 56
Russell, Bertrand 122
Rutherford, Mark 105

'Sailing to Byzantium' 46
Saint-Évermond, Charles de 130
Sandy, Mark 54
Sarah (wife of Abraham) 55
Sartre, Jean-Paul 7, 28-29, 122
Satire III (Donne's) 148
Saturn 144
Savage, Richard 15-16, 148
Scott, Walter 67
Sebastian, Saint 150
Senescence: The Last Half of Life 147
Sense and Sensibility 84
Sentenced to Life 95, 108
Seven Samurai, The 32
Seward, Anna 127
Shakespeare, Ann 19
Shakespeare, Judith 18
Shakespeare, Susannah 18
Shakespeare, William 10, 16-18, 21-22, 27, 28, 31, 32, 65-6, 68, 85, 93, 102, 107, 114, 120, 132, 133, 134, 139, 140, 142
Shelley, Percy Bysshe 65, 66, 71, 73, 84, 136
'Simon Lee' 53-4, 75, 92
Simonides 147
Sinatra, Frank 101, 103
Small, Helen 7, 9, 145-146
Smart, Jeffrey 101,103
'Smocking Block, The' 96
Socrates 43, 45
Somewhere Towards the End 39

'Sonnet 29, Shakespeare's' 102
'Sonnet 55, Shakespeare's' 65
'Sonnet 73, Shakespeare's 28
Sonnets, Shakespeare's 28
Sophocles 28, 43, 45, 147
Sorescu, Martin 116
Southey, Robert 126-127
'Spur, The' 46
Staël, Madame de 104
Steinach, Eugen 47
Stendhal 44, 66-67, 68, 71, 83, 95, 102, 103
Sterne, Laurence 114
Stet 113
Stevens, Major Charles Henry 116
Stone, Lawrence 23-4, 25
Stoppard, Tom 150
Stories of Ageing 5
'Superannuated Man, The' 24
Swift, Jonathan 33-35, 40-41, 42, 44, 80, 98, 132

Tale of a Tub, The 33
Tallis, Raymond 4
Taunton, Nina 5, 146
Tempest, The 17, 19
Thane, Pat 3-5, 6, 27
Thomas, Dylan 25
Thomas, Keith 22-3, 32, 51
Thompson, Denys 3
Thunberg, Greta 142
Tithonus 33-34
Tolstoy, Leo 120-121, 122
Tom Jones 65
Tomalin, Claire 114
Tono-Bungay 116
Tower, The 46
Tristram Shandy 114
Troilus and Cressida 32
Trollope, Anthony 80, 81

Ulysses 61, 68, 135-136
Unreliable Memoirs 95

Vanity of Human Wishes, The 105
Victorians and Old Age, The 5
Visionary Dreariness, The 11
Vision of Judgment, The 126
Volpone 75-77, 132

Voltaire 18, 66
Voronoff, Serge 47

Wada, Shuichi 33
Waiting for Godot 133
Walpole, Horace 130
Walters, Julie 42
Walton, Izaak 72
Washington Square 59, 82
Way of the World, The 42
Wellington, Duke of 8
Wells, H. G. 70, 116, 117
Wheeler, Margaret 18
Wild Ass's Skin, The 120
Wilde, Oscar 40, 128,
Wilson, John Dover 66
Wiltshire, John 114
Within a Budding Grove 16
Wolpert, Lewis 31

Women in Love 35, 129
Women Writers and Old Age 5
Wood, Victoria 42
Wood, Wee Georgie 143
Woodward, Kathleen 30-31, 97
Wordsworth and the Question of
    Ageing' 54
Wordsworth, Dorothy 51
Wordsworth, William 10, 51-55, 58, 63,
    65, 66, 70, 72, 75, 92, 96, 102, 105, 110,
    114, 115, 136
World of William Clissold, The 116
Wrinkled Deep in Time 10

Yeats, W. B. 45-46, 47
Yeats: The Man and the Mask 47

Zeno 150
Zola, Émile 79

You may also be interested in:

The Older Liszt

Music, World and Spirit

by Peter Coleman

Franz Liszt is well known for his early years as 'super-star' pianist who excited audiences throughout Europe, but his later life is also of great interest. In his final 25 years he sought to achieve his life's aims of promoting new forms of music and giving stronger witness to his Christian faith, while continuing to support his stalwart life partner Princess Carolyne. However, he was to face unexpected problems in the continued negative reception of his music and recrimination in his closest relationship.

Drawing on detailed analysis of Liszt's correspondence from his fiftieth year onwards, Peter Coleman approaches his later life as a case study of an older person grappling with a succession of often disturbing life experiences. These included the deaths of two of his children, political upheaval and war within Europe, and a growing realisation of his own past failings. Liszt suffered frequent bouts of depression but never ceased composing music nor steadfastly heeding Christ's command to bear one's cross. This sensitive treatment of an extraordinary individual will appeal to the scholar and general reader alike.

> *Liszt's deep-rooted desire to serve his God and his Church through music and in a well-lived life was a notion too esoteric for most of his male colleagues. His self-scrutiny in an array of later correspondence is acutely probed in this wonderfully sensitive account of Liszt's final decades.* – **Leslie Howard**

Peter Coleman is a psychologist and gerontologist specialising in the interplay between ageing, spirituality and mental health. He is Emeritus Professor of Psycho-Gerontology at the University of Southampton, and has co-authored numerous books including *Belief and Ageing: Spiritual Pathways in Later Life* and *Self and Meaning in the Lives of Older People*. Love of Liszt's music led him to join the Liszt Society while still a teenager and he has continued to read widely about Liszt's life.

Published 2023

Hardback ISBN: 978 0 7188 9715 4
Paperback ISBN: 978 0 7188 9713 0
PDF ISBN: 978 0 7188 9714 7
ePub ISBN: 978 0 7188 9712 3

You may also be interested in:

The Business of Reading

A Hundred Years of the English Novel

by Julian Lovelock

In *The Business of Reading*, Julian Lovelock charts the development of the English novel over the past hundred years. Smuggling in titles from Scotland, Ireland and the Caribbean, he focuses on twenty texts written since the end of the First World War, some well-known but others less so, placing them in their historical context. Novelists represented range from D.H. Lawrence, E.M. Forster and Virginia Woolf, through Graham Greene, Kingsley Amis and Iris Murdoch, to such contemporary writers as Ian McEwan, Maggie O'Farrell and Graham Swift.

Written in a lucid style that reflects his expertise and enthusiasm, Lovelock's innovative selection, perceptive analysis and lightness of touch will appeal to the general reader, the book club member and the student. He argues that our response as readers is an important part of the creative process, and while he mainly avoids the critical '-isms' that have characterised recent academic debate, he introduces such concepts as intertextuality, metafiction and the role of the often unreliable narrator, showing how an appreciation of the way the language of fiction works can only add to our understanding and enjoyment.

> 'The author's enthusiasm and knowledge seeps through on every page and he weaves together connections between the texts which will help trigger many a pleasurable discussion about the business of reading.'
> **– D.H. Lawrence Society**

Julian Lovelock has spent his life in education, as a teacher, headmaster and university lecturer. He is now a Senior Research Fellow in the Department of English at the University of Buckingham, where he was previously Dean of Arts and Languages and Pro Vice-Chancellor. His many publications include *Swallows, Amazons and Coots: A Reading of Arthur Ransome* (2016) and *From Morality to Mayhem: The Fall and Rise of the English School Story* (2018), both published by The Lutterworth Press.

Published 2022

Paperback ISBN: 978 0 7188 9595 2
PDF ISBN: 978 0 7188 9596 9
ePub ISBN: 978 0 7188 9597 6

You may also be interested in:

The Story of the Novel

by George Watson

As George Watson playfully observes, the story is the best thing about a novel. The deliberately ambiguous title of his book reflects the fact that it combines a study of the art of narrative with the history of the novel as a literary form, since its emergence some three centuries ago.

Employing a thematic approach, the author moves from one aspect of narrative to another rather than discussing novelists chronologically. The book considers various kinds of novels, such as the memoir novel and discusses issues such as the presentation of dialogue, the creation of scenes, tense and time and the relationship between the novel and history.

Arguments are illustrated by well-known rather than obscure works, or novels likely to be familiar to students who take this book as a starting-point for the modern study of narrative. The reader is presented with a clear picture of how the novel has evolved and how its chief conventions have developed and changed since the seventeenth century.

This new and revised edition brings back to life this invaluable and straightforward work on the technique of the novel, which first appeared in 1979.

> *'The author's enthusiasm and knowledge seeps through on every page and he weaves together connections between the texts which will help trigger many a pleasurable discussion about the business of reading.'*
> **– D.H. Lawrence Society**

George Watson was Fellow in English at St John's College, Cambridge, and had been Sandars Reader in Bibliography. He published a number of books on literature and political thought, including *The Literary Critics*, and was general editor of the *New Cambridge Bibliography of English Literature*. His other publications with the Lutterworth Press include: *Lost Literature of Socialism* (1st Edition 1998, 2nd Edition 2010); *Never Ones for Theory? England and the War of Ideas* (2001); *The English Ideology: Studies on the Language of Victorian Politics* (2004); *Take Back the Past: Myths of the Twentieth Century* (2007); and *Heresies and Heretics: Memories of the Twentieth Century* (2013). He died in 2013.

Published 2008

Paperback ISBN: 978 0 7188 3094 6